Differentiation, RTI, and Achievement

How They Work Together

Carolyn Coil

Pieces of Learning

CLC0455
© 2009 Pieces of Learning
Marion IL
ISBN 978-1-934358-49-8
Printed by McNaughton & Gunn Inc, Saline MI
10/2010

Acknowledgements

As with every book, I could not have completed this without help from many people. Special thanks to:

- Mona Livermont, my office assistant and good friend, who worked tirelessly on the formatting and computer graphics in this book.

- Kathy Balsamo, my editor and good friend, for suggestions and resources and for encouraging me to complete this book in a timely manner!

- Dr. Lynn Grady, former colleague and good friend, for her wise explanations about struggling readers and interventions that could help them.

- Doug Coil, my husband and constant support, for understanding as I worked many, many hours in my office at home to get this finished!

Dedication

To all teachers ---

Your work is challenging, daunting, exciting and exhausting! Your dedication is an inspiration to me and many others.

I hope this book will give you some practical tools to use in helping every child grow and reach his or her greatest potential.

Table of Contents

Introduction 6

Curriculum Compacting 19
    Vignette: Caroline 20
    Curriculum Compactor: Math.................................. 21
    Curriculum Compacting RTI example..................... 22
    Curriculum Compacting RTI form 25

Fear of Failure 28
    Vignette: Anthony 29
    Anthony's Behavioral Characteristics Checklist. 30
    Worst Case Scenario Activity................................ 31
    Fear of Failure RTI example 32
    Fear of Failure RTI form 35

Goal Setting 38
    Vignette: Shane 39
    "What Can You Learn from the World of Sports?" 40
    Lifeline Activity... 41
    Goal Setting RTI example 42
    Goal Setting RTI form 45

Graphic Organizers 48
    Vignette: Sophia 49
    Graphic Organizers RTI example 50
    Graphic Organizers RTI form.............................. 53

Group Work 56
    Vignette: Isabella 57
    Flexible Grouping Patterns 58
    Listening Skills Checklist 59
    Group Work RTI example 60
    Group Work RTI form 63

Learning Preferences 66
    Vignette: Madison.. 67
    Madison's Learning Preferences Checklist............................ 68
    Animal Habitats ILP™ 69
    Animal Habitats Mini-Rubric 70
    Learning Preferences RTI example 71
    Learning Preferences RTI form 74

Negative Peer Pressure **77**
    Vignette: Melinda... 78
    Melinda's Behavioral Characteristics Checklist 79
    Negative Peer Pressure RTI example 80
    Negative Peer Pressure RTI form....................................... 83

Number Sense **86**
    Vignette: Mia.. 87
    Number Sense RTI example 88
    Number Sense RTI form.. 91

Organizational Skills..**94**
    Vignette: Jack... 95
    Jack's RTI Organization Checklist...................................... 96
    Interventions to Help Develop Organizational Skills 97
    School Supplies Checklist 98
    Organizational Skills RTI example...................................... 99
    Organizational Skills RTI form 102

Sequencing Skills...**105**
    Vignette: Jose... 106
    Sequencing Skills Interventions.. 107
    Sequencing Skills RTI example 108
    Sequencing Skills RTI form 111

Test-Taking Skills...**114**
    Vignette: Jermaine..................................... 115
    Jermaine's Achievement Characteristics Checklist 116
    Test-Taking Skills (Memorization Techniques) RTI example.. 117
    Test-Taking Skills (Memorization Techniques) RTI form 120

Tiered Lessons and Units...**123**
    Vignette: Noah and Logan... 124
    Compound Words Tiered Lesson Plan................................. 125
    Tiered Lesson Level 1 RTI example 127
    Tiered Lesson Level 1 RTI form 130
    Tiered Lesson Level 3 RTI example 133
    Tiered Lesson Level 3 RTI form 136

© Pieces of Learning

RTI Blank Forms..**139**

  Blank RTI Form 140
  Comprehension Skills: Listening and Speaking..................... 143
  Comprehension Skills: Reading and Writing 146
  Math Problem Solving 149
  Phonemic Awareness 152
  Self-Esteem/Self-Confidence.................................. 155
  Spelling/Vocabulary Patterns................................. 158
  Test-Taking Skills: Following Directions 161
  Test-Taking Skills: Multiple Choice techniques.................... 164
  Test-Taking Skills: Reading the Questions 167
  Test-Taking Skills: Time Management 170

Other Reproducible Forms..**173**

  Curriculum Compactor.. 174
  Goal Setting: Where Do You Want To Go –
  How Do You Plan To Get There? 175
  Mindmap – Goal Setting, Problem Solving and
      Decision Making 176
  Concept Map 177
  Storyboard Visual Organizer.................................. 178
  Compare/Contrast - Venn Diagram 179
  Learning Preferences Checklist 180
  Learning Styles Checklist 181
  Learning Modalities Checklist 182
  Listening Skills Checklist 184
  RTI Achievement Characteristics Checklist...................... 185
  RTI Behavioral Characteristics Checklist....................... 186
  RTI Organization Checklist 187
  Tiered Lesson Planning....................................... 188
  Individual Lesson Plan™ 192
  ILP™ Assessment form 195
  Product Criteria Cards 196

Afterword **199**

Introduction

What should teachers do to meet the needs of all the students in their classrooms, including those who seem to be struggling academically or behaviorally? What can we do to help underachievers so that they don't fall behind? How do we handle behavior problems in a positive and proactive way? What can we do to challenge our brightest students? How do we know when our best classroom strategies are not working? How do we decide when it is appropriate for some students to be referred for special education or other special services? Finally, how do we obtain the data and information necessary to make such decisions in a professional and accurate way?

The answers to these questions revolve around three basic educational ideas – differentiation, achievement, and response to intervention (RTI). In this book you will see how these three ideas are interrelated, how they work together, and how we can help all of our students when we implement practical research-based classroom strategies and interventions based on them.

It is important to determine why a specific student is a low achiever in school. What factors are causing poor academic performance? It is equally important to determine if a student is sitting in class learning nothing new while he waits for everyone else to catch up. Differentiating instruction to meet the needs of all students is one of the basics for 21st century teachers. The next step, however, is to find out if what we are doing is really working to raise the achievement of an individual student or group of students.

The RTI approach helps us learn what works and what doesn't. Some students need interventions that deal with specific academic skill deficits. Others need motivation or organizational skills or help with appropriate classroom behavior. Thinking strategies and interventions can aid students who need help in reading, writing, math, and problem solving. Students who are behavior problems may need strategies in self-discipline and behavior management.

In this book you will learn about a variety of research-based interventions including both behavioral/classroom management strategies and academic/ instructional strategies. You will find out how to link student needs to specific interventions, thereby selecting the right interventions to meet the needs of each student.

Use this book as you collaborate with other teachers. Follow a structured problem solving process to discover the best interventions for specific students. Use multi-disciplinary teams – sometimes called student assistance teams or student support teams – to work together brainstorming specific strategies and interventions for success. In general, it is best to try positive preliminary intervention strategies first. Normally these are good classroom management and differentiation strategies.

Most importantly, this book will help you learn how to assess and monitor individual student progress and how to select and use the *Coil RTI Progress Monitoring Forms*™ that best meet your needs and the needs of your students.

RESPONSE TO INTERVENTION

Response to Intervention (RTI) began as a special education initiative that emphasizes the need for prevention strategies in the regular classroom. It was originally conceived as a way to help struggling students before they were referred for special education services and identified as having learning disabilities. This need was emphasized in the 2004 reauthorization of the Individuals with Disabilities Education Act (IDEA).

It recommends intervention services and the use of research-based best practices and strategies in the general education classroom <u>before</u> a referral for special education services. Interventions generally are those classroom practices that have been demonstrated to be effective for most students.

The two most common ways to implement RTI are:

1. The Problem Solving Approach

    This approach uses a team to brainstorm interventions and strategies to meet each student's individual needs. In this approach, the team identifies the problem or problems, determines potential causes, and then develops an individualized plan to deal with the problem. A variety of different interventions may be considered. These interventions remain flexible based on individual needs and the student's response when the intervention is tried. When interventions are selected, they may be implemented by the general education teacher, a tutor, paraprofessional, or specialist depending upon the Tier of service.

2. The Standard Treatment Approach

    This approach uses the same interventions for many different students who have similar needs. These interventions are research-based and delivered in a standardized format. They can address one or more academic or behavioral needs. Those who prefer a standard treatment protocol point to greater quality control as the main advantage to this approach. This approach has been used predominantly in research studies.

In this book we will consider research-based strategies, methods, and techniques to help individual teachers, student support teams, administrators, and other educators who are using the Problem Solving Approach.

THE RTI TRIANGULAR TIERED MODEL

RTI has often been thought of as a three-tiered triangular model with more intensive interventions needed at each tier.

Tier 1 consists of high quality instruction for all students. The progress of targeted students is monitored frequently, but the types of instruction and services they receive are the same as all other students in the classroom. Targeted students may have more time for instruction or may have instruction more frequently. In any case, all students in the regular education classroom have access to appropriate instruction and worthwhile learning experiences.

Tier 2 gives more support to students who have not made adequate progress or who are considered unresponsive in Tier 1. They are moved to Tier 2 which can be different in content or rigor. The interventions in this Tier can be individualized (Problem Solving approach) or standardized (Standard Treatment approach) as described above.

Tier 3 consists of more intensive and concentrated interventions and may result in referral for special education services.

RTI AND GIFTED STUDENTS

Like many good ideas in education, RTI has now been adapted to other types of students beyond those students it was originally designed to help. It has value for a variety of different types of students because it provides a framework for responding to the needs of all students in the regular classroom.
The RTI approach, which includes problem solving, quality assessments, research-based individualized strategies, differentiated curriculum, pre-assessment, formative assessment and progress monitoring, is an approach that can benefit gifted and high-ability students as well as struggling students. Reasons include:

- Gifted students often need targeted interventions so that they do not become bored with school or become mental drop-outs.
- Gifted students who can achieve well beyond grade level need interventions to assure that they continue to grow and progress academically.
- Unmotivated gifted students need interventions to keep them focused, interested, and alert.
- Gifted underachievers often need interventions in both behavioral and academic areas.
- Gifted students may also have disabilities, may be learning English as a second language, or may have other academic or behavioral issues that need special attention.

Considering gifted and other highly able students within the RTI approach, I along with others believe a more accurate model than the triangular model is a diamond with Tier 1 in the middle and Tiers 2 and 3 going in both directions. This should be seen as a flexible and fluid model in both directions with the Tiers seen as a back-and-forth continuum rather than a rigid step-by-step process.

We need to move beyond thinking of RTI as a Special Education initiative to thinking about it as an approach to use with many different types of students.

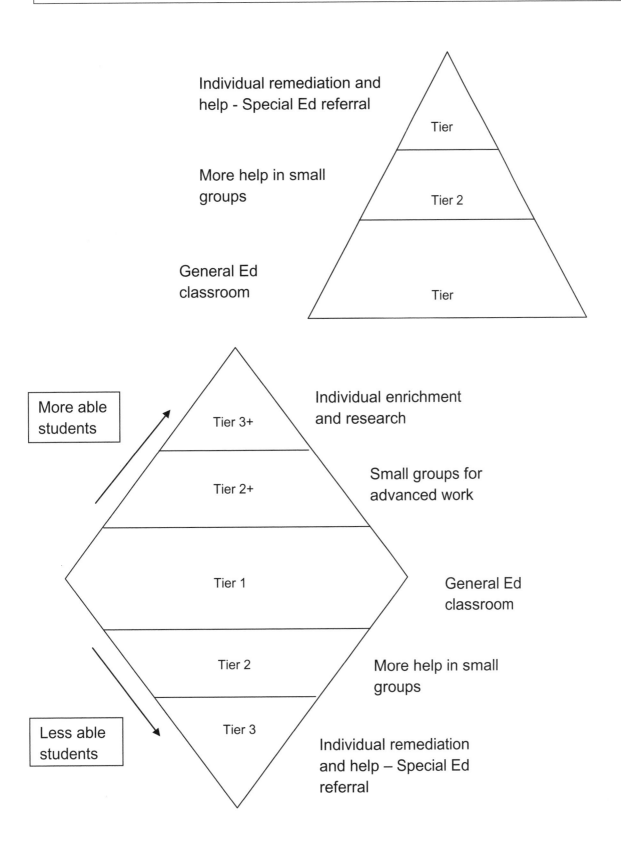

Individual remediation and help - Special Ed referral

Tier

More help in small groups

Tier 2

General Ed classroom

Tier

More able students

Tier 3+

Individual enrichment and research

Tier 2+

Small groups for advanced work

Tier 1

General Ed classroom

Tier 2

More help in small groups

Tier 3

Less able students

Individual remediation and help – Special Ed referral

RTI and Assessment

The RTI approach should include both student assessment/monitoring and specific interventions appropriate for that child. In the RTI approach, schools are likely to have:

- Academic and behavioral screening for all students – some form of school-wide assessment for all students
- Targeted interventions aimed at addressing individual student's problem areas and needs that were identified during the screening process
- Frequent monitoring of student progress in order to assess how well a specific intervention is working

Make use of pre-assessments before beginning any academic activity in order to determine individual student needs. Pre-assessment is:

- an essential element of differentiation and RTI
- necessary in order to meet the diverse needs of each student
- a way to specify each student's starting point before instruction begins

Pre-assessment shows learning differences among students (important for differentiation) and indicates when there is a need for targeted interventions (important for RTI).

Using specific strategies and interventions with individual students is the next step. Because the RTI process involves gathering and evaluating assessment data, you must also monitor the interventions. This is the formative assessment phase of RTI. Formative assessment is:

- assessment while instruction and/or student work is going on
- assessment to inform teachers, parents, and/or students about the effectiveness of the instruction/intervention
- a way to show student progress toward a learning goal (RTI progress monitoring)

Formative assessment can alert teachers to a student's misunderstandings about the knowledge or skill being taught. It often gives evidence of a student's need to learn something again or in a different way, and conversely can show that a student has already mastered the material being taught. It can thereby guide decision-making concerning the next step in the instructional process.

During the intervention process, measure student progress often. Close monitoring will advise you if the intervention is working or not. Use multiple data sources to monitor student progress. Many schools have adopted one of a number of computerized testing instruments that can quickly show student progress through line graphs, bar graphs, or charts. These are useful tools, but do not think you are "doing RTI" if all you do is an intervention and print out a computerized graph once every six weeks! Using multiple data sources is the key to implementing RTI effectively.

You may want to use daily or weekly report cards for student behavior, academic gains, work habits, effort, and organization. Use rubrics with rating scales that show progress toward a goal. Use checklists for behavioral goals such as organization, staying on task, paying attention, completing work, etc.

There is no standardized method of assessing a student's response to an intervention. It is usually based on some measurement of performance at the end of the intervention and/or a measurement of growth/progress over time. Because progress monitoring generally is considered to be a key factor in implementing RTI effectively, this book has many RTI Progress Monitoring Forms to help you do this well.

COIL RTI PROGRESS MONITORING FORMS™

The *Coil RTI Progress Monitoring Forms™* that you will see throughout this book all have the same basic structure. Each focuses on a different behavior, academic skill, or strategy/intervention.

Follow the procedure described below to use any of the forms effectively. See the blank form on the next three pages to guide you through this procedure.

1. Check the title at the top of each *Coil RTI Progress Monitoring Form™* to find one that focuses on the behavior, knowledge, skill, or intervention you are addressing.

2. Use pre-assessments to determine individual student needs. Record the results on the first page of the appropriate *Coil RTI Progress Monitoring Form™*.

3. Next link student needs with specific research-based interventions and strategies. Write the planned intervention or interventions on the bottom of the first page of the appropriate *Coil RTI Progress Monitoring Form™*.

4. Use page 2 of the appropriate *Coil RTI Progress Monitoring Form™* to measure and record student progress often during the intervention process. Close monitoring will let you know if the intervention is working or not. You may duplicate page 2 as many times as is needed to monitor the intervention successfully.

5. Use page 3 of the form as you decide if the intervention has or has not been successful. Look for improvement from the starting point of the intervention. Assessments of progress and ways to determine whether to stop or continue the intervention are both important in this process.

Because progress in many of the targeted behaviors and skills cannot be determined by a test score alone, it is important to use other assessment methods as well. Assessments noted on the *Coil RTI Progress Monitoring Form™* include:

- Test scores
- Observations
- Checklists and rating scales
- Performance assessments (rubrics)

Coil RTI Progress Monitoring Form™

Need/Concern or Intervention _____

1

Student's Name _____

Targeted Skill, Knowledge, or Behavior

Pre-assessment: *(Record all that apply)*

Date(s) of Pre-assessment _____

Test score(s) _____   Checklist Indicator(s) _____

Observation(s)

2

Performance Assessment

Below expectation..Exceeds Expectations

Strategies or Interventions *(Describe or list below)*

Intervention or Strategy   **Person Responsible**   **Timeline**

3

Formative Assessments *(Monitoring the Student's Response to the Intervention*

Date _____

Test score _____   Checklist Indicator(s) _____

Observation(s)

Performance Assessment
Below expectation..Exceeds Expectations

Date _____

Test score _____   Checklist Indicator(s) _____

Observation(s)

4

Performance Assessment
Below expectation..Exceeds Expectations

Date _____

Test score _____   Checklist Indicator(s) _____

Observation(s)

Performance Assessment
Below expectation..Exceeds Expectations

Summarize the Student's Response to the Intervention(s)

5

Decision:

☐ Successfully mastered the targeted skill, knowledge or behavior. Targeted intervention no longer needed.

☐ Continue the same intervention(s) as needed and appropriate

☐ Modify the intervention:

☐ Select / implement a new intervention

☐ Move to the next tier (Tier _____)

☐ Refer for Special Education evaluation or other special services:

DIFFERENTIATION & RTI: CONNECTIONS

> *When we see huge disparities in achievement among students of the same age and grade, it is hard to understand what the frequently used phrase 'being on grade level' means. Across the United States, students in every grade fall at different points in an achievement range that starts very high and ends very low; there is nothing "level" about it.*
>
> **— Barton & Coley, Educational Leadership,**
> **December 2008-January 2009**

The above quote shows the need for differentiation in every classroom. The RTI approach points the way to individualized, differentiated instruction for all students along with continuous formative assessment so that we can readily see which strategies work with an individual student and which do not. Differentiation and the RTI approach work hand-in-hand to bring all students to success. Implementing a scientifically-based differentiated curriculum using differentiated instructional strategies is essential for RTI.

Ideas to consider when thinking about connections between RTI and Differentiation:

- Differentiation provides the classroom structure that makes RTI doable.
- Differentiation helps students who learn in different ways; RTI depends on this happening.
- The Interventions (the 'I') in RTI = Differentiation Strategies
- Differentiation strategies are flexible and are designed to meet individual needs; the RTI problem-solving approach is based on flexible, individual interventions.
- Differentiation and the RTI approach assume that "one-size-fits-all" curriculum really fits no one.
- RTI and Differentiation both rely on pre-assessment and formative assessment.
- RTI and Differentiation focus on students' progress toward learning goals.
- RTI and Differentiation lead students to understand their own learning preferences.
- Differentiation (originated in Gifted Education) and RTI (originated in Special Education) both focus on students whose needs are different from the average.

MOTIVATION, ACHIEVEMENT & RTI: CONNECTIONS

RTI does not just focus on academic problems. An important element of RTI involves behavioral interventions. In the tiered system of RTI, behavioral interventions can be looked at in this way:

Tier 1 – Schoolwide and classroom behavior management strategies

Tier 2 – Specific, targeted social behavior interventions generally in a small group setting

Tier 3 – Intensive and focused on individual behavioral deficits. This may include individual counseling

Some students need help in understanding and complying with the behavioral expectations of the school. Others need to learn to take responsibility for their own actions. The goal of behavioral interventions is for students to exhibit positive behaviors that lead to success and achievement in school. Many students have the academic ability to succeed in school but do not because of their own behavior.

Motivation, achievement, and behavior in school are linked. Consider the following:

- Behavior problems are often caused by a lack of motivation. RTI provides a way to look at possible causes and monitor interventions to determine if they work in improving both behavior and motivation.
- Low self-esteem, fear of failure, negative peer pressure, and a lack of self-confidence result in behaviors that lead to doing poor work in school. The RTI approach helps in targeting such behaviors and providing interventions to deal with them.
- Low achievement may stem from lack of organization, time management, test-taking, or study skills. Specific interventions to meet these needs can be planned, implemented, and monitored through the RTI approach.

HOW TO USE THIS BOOK

This book gives you many practical RTI Progress Monitoring Forms on a variety of behaviors, knowledge, skills, and interventions. In each of the categories below, you will find:
- a vignette of a student
- an example of the Coil RTI Progress Monitoring Form ™ used with this student
- any other documentation, checklists, or assessment forms that were used with this student
- a blank RTI form of the same type for you to use with your students

- – Curriculum Compacting

- – Fear of Failure

- – Goal Setting

- – Graphic Organizers

- – Group Work

- – Learning Preferences

- – Negative Peer Pressure

- – Number Sense

- – Organizational Skills

- – Sequencing Skills

- – Test-Taking Skills: Memorization

- – Tiered Lessons (Levels 1 & 3)

OTHER READY-TO-USE FORMS

In addition, you will find ready-to-use Coil RTI Progress Monitoring Forms ™ beginning on page 134 in the following categories:

- ❑ Comprehension skills: Listening and Speaking
- ❑ Comprehension skills: Reading and Writing
- ❑ Math Problem Solving
- ❑ Phonemic Awareness
- ❑ Self Confidence
- ❑ Spelling/Vocabulary Patterns
- ❑ Test-Taking Skills: Following Directions
- ❑ Test-Taking Skills: Multiple Choice techniques
- ❑ Test-Taking Skills: Reading the Questions
- ❑ Test-Taking Skills: Time Management

You will also find beginning on page 173 the following ready-to-use forms and assessment checklists:

- ❑ Curriculum Compactor
- ❑ Goal Setting: Where Do You Want To Go – How Do You Plan To Get There?
- ❑ Mindmap – Goal Setting, Problem Solving and Decision Making
- ❑ Concept Map
- ❑ Storyboard Visual Organizer
- ❑ Compare/Contrast - Venn diagram
- ❑ Learning Preferences Checklist
- ❑ Learning Styles Checklist
- ❑ Learning Modalities Checklist
- ❑ Listening Skills Checklist
- ❑ RTI Achievement Characteristics Checklist
- ❑ RTI Behavioral Characteristics Checklist
- ❑ RTI Organization Checklist
- ❑ Tiered Lesson Planning form
- ❑ Individual Lesson Plan™ form and ILP™ Assessment form
- ❑ Criteria Cards – samples and blank form

Curriculum Compacting

VIGNETTE: CAROLINE

CURRICULUM COMPACTOR: MATH

CURRICULUM COMPACTING RTI EXAMPLE

CURRICULUM COMPACTING RTI FORM

CAROLINE

Caroline is a high achieving student who generally knows most of the skills and knowledge in her grade level's math and reading standards. She is a teacher-pleaser and rarely complains that the work is boring or too easy. However, she has developed the habit of being a rather dependent learner and waits for teacher approval on everything she does in school.

Caroline is an excellent candidate for the Curriculum Compacting strategy. In Curriculum Compacting, a research-based strategy developed by Dr. Joseph Renzulli at the University of Connecticut, skills and knowledge that can be easily tested are identified. Mastery level is established by the classroom teacher, and alternate activities are delineated.

The Curriculum Compactor form has three columns:

Column 1:   Skill, Knowledge, Benchmark, or Standard
Column 2:   Documentation of Mastery
Column 3:   Alternate Activities

The basic goal of this strategy is to challenge high-ability students rather than having them do the regular classroom work while learning little that is new. Students generally take pre-tests before the beginning of a unit of instruction. If mastery is attained, they work on alternate activities while the rest of the class is learning the skill or knowledge.

This differentiation strategy encourages good organization and time management skills. It leads students to becoming more responsible for their own learning. Usually the classroom teacher establishes a time each day to meet with compacting students in order to answer their questions, offer suggestions, and give them additional guidance. The classroom teacher, however, is generally not available consistently during the learning process, and some independence in learning is both expected and encouraged.

As you can see from Caroline's *Coil RTI Progress Monitoring Form™*, she demonstrated mastery of multiplication of one digit numbers. Because of this, she was able to work on an alternate activity that developed higher-level thinking skills and challenged her to use her knowledge in a new way. Because we monitored her progress, we could readily see that while her basic math skills are very good, she needs more help in learning to work independently.

On the next page, you can see Caroline's Curriculum Compactor form. A blank Curriculum Compactor form for you to complete with your students is found on page 25.

CURRICULUM COMPACTOR FORM

Student's Name _____Caroline_____

Skill, Knowledge, Benchmark, or Standard	Documentation of Mastery	Student Choice Alternate Activities
All single digit multiplication facts up to 9 x 9	Pretest of all facts with a score of 90% or above	1. Write a story called "The Land with No Multiplication." or 2. Create a card game that requires both skill in multiplication and logical thinking. or 3. Your choice of activity with teach er approval

Coil RTI Progress Monitoring Form™
Curriculum Compacting

Student's Name _____Caroline_____

Targeted Skill, Knowledge, or Behavior

- Academic skills/knowledge that are easily assessed
  (Targeted skill/knowledge: Multiplication facts through 9 x 9

- Student claims to be "bored" and says she already knows the work

Pre-assessment: (Record all that apply)

Date(s) of Pre-assessment _____

Test score(s) 100% on pretest   Checklist Indicator(s) _____

Observation(s)

Pretest covered all multiplication facts up to 9 x 9.

Performance Assessment
Below Expectation...Exceeds Expectations

Student has an understanding of some of the skills/ knowledge and could compact out of some of the work.	Student has an understanding of almost all of the skills/ knowledge and could usually compact out and do alternate activities.	Student has an understanding of all the skills/knowledge for this unit and could compact out of the entire unit and do alternate activities.	Student has mastered all the skills/knowledge for this unit but has problems working independently doing higher level alternate activities.	Student has mastered all the skills/ knowledge for this unit and works well independently doing higher level alternate learning activities.

Strategies or Interventions: (Describe or list below)

Use the Curriculum Compacting strategy with this student. She will have a choice between two alternate activities or can come up with her own activity with teacher approval. Alternate activity choices:

1. Write a story entitled "The Land with No Multiplication." Be creative but include what you know about multiplication and its uses. Explain what might happen if people didn't know how to multiply.

2. Create a card game that requires both skill in multiplication and logical thinking. Make the game and write the rules. Then play it with a classmate.

Formative Assessments *(Monitoring the Student's Response to Curriculum Compacting)*

Date __Monday____

Test score _____ Checklist Indicator(s) _____

Observation(s)

Caroline chooses to write a story called "The Land with No Multiplication."

Performance Assessment

Below Expectation...Exceeds Expectations

| Student has an understanding of some of the skills/ knowledge and could compact out of some of the work. | Student has an understanding of almost all of the skills/ knowledge and could usually compact out and do alternate activities. | Student has an understanding of all the skills/knowledge for this unit and could compact out of the entire unit and do alternate activities. | Student has mastered all the skills/ knowledge for this unit but has problems working independently doing higher level alternate activities. | Student has mastered all the skills/ knowledge for this unit and works well independently doing higher level alternate learning activities. |

Date __Tuesday-Friday___

Test score _____ Checklist Indicator(s) Checkpoint with teacher each day

Observation(s)

Caroline has difficulty working independently. Needs lots of guidance in writing the story.

Performance Assessment

Below Expectation...Exceeds Expectations

| Student has an understanding of some of the skills/ knowledge and could compact out of some of the work. | Student has an understanding of some of the skills/ knowledge and could compact out of some of the work. | Student has an understanding of all the skills/knowledge for this unit and could compact out of the entire unit and do alternate activities. | Student has mastered all the skills/ knowledge for this unit but has problems working independently doing higher level alternate activities. | Student has mastered all the skills/ knowledge for this unit and works well independently doing higher level alternate learning activities. |

Date __Monday of 2nd week____

Test score 100% on post test   Checklist Indicator(s) _____

Observation(s)

Caroline remains above mastery level in multiplication facts. Completed the story. Needs to develop skills in independent learning.

Performance Assessment

Below Expectation...Exceeds Expectations

| Student has an understanding of some of the skills/ knowledge and could compact out of some of the work. | Student has an understanding of almost all of the skills/ knowledge and could usually compact out and do alternate activities. | Student has an understanding of all the skills/knowledge for this unit and could compact out of the entire unit and do alternate activities. | Student has mastered all the skills/ knowledge for this unit but has problems working independently doing higher level alternate activities. | Student has mastered all the skills/ knowledge for this unit and works well independently doing higher level alternate learning activities. |

Summarize the Student's Response to Curriculum Compacting

1. Caroline exceeded grade level mastery in multiplication skills.

2. Story challenged her to develop higher-level thinking skills (application, analysis, synthesis, and evaluation).

3. Needs to work on independent learning skills.

4. She worked on the curriculum compacting alternate activity for one week.

Decision:

X Continue curriculum compacting as needed and appropriate

☐ Modify the intervention:

X Select / implement a new intervention
Work on developing skills in independent learning.

☐ Move to the next tier (Tier _____)

☐ Refer for other special services:

Coil RTI Progress Monitoring Form™
Curriculum Compacting

Student's Name _____

Targeted Skill, Knowledge, or Behavior
- **Academic skills/knowledge that are easily assessed (Targeted skill/knowledge: _____)**

- **Student claims to be "bored" and says he already knows the work**

Pre-assessment: *(Record all that apply)*

Date(s) of Pre-assessment _____

Test score(s) _____ Checklist Indicator(s) _____

Observation(s) _____

Performance Assessment

Below Expectation..Exceeds Expectations

Student has an understanding of some of the skills/ knowledge and could compact out of some of the work.	Student has an understanding of almost all of the skills/ knowledge and could usually compact out and do alternate activities	Student has an understanding of all the skills/knowledge for this unit and could compact out of the entire unit and do alternate activities.	Student has mastered all the skills/ knowledge for this unit but has problems working independently doing higher level alternate activities.	Student has mastered all the skills/ knowledge for this unit and works well independently doing higher level alternate learning activities.

Strategies or Interventions: *(Describe or list below)*

Intervention or Strategy   **Person Responsible**   **Timeline**

Formative Assessments *(Monitoring the Student's Response to Curriculum Compacting)*

Date _____

Test score _____ Checklist Indicator(s) _____

Observation(s)

Performance Assessment
Below Expectation...Exceeds Expectations

Student has an understanding of some of the skills/ knowledge and could compact out of some of the work.	Student has an understanding of almost all of the skills/ knowledge and could usually compact out and do alternate activities.	Student has an understanding of all the skills/knowledge for this unit and could compact out of the entire unit and do alternate activities.	Student has mastered all the skills/ knowledge for this unit but has problems working independently doing higher level alternate activities.	Student has mastered all the skills/ knowledge for this unit and works well independently doing higher level alternate learning activities.

Date _____

Test score _____ Checklist Indicator(s) _____

Observation(s)

Performance Assessment
Below Expectation...Exceeds Expectations

Student has an understanding of some of the skills/ knowledge and could compact out of some of the work.	Student has an understanding of almost all of the skills/ knowledge and could usuallly compact out and do alernate activities.	Student has an understanding of all the skills/knowledge for this unit and could compact out of the entire unit and do alternate activities.	Student has mastered all the skills/ knowledge for this unit but has problems working independently doing higher level alternate activities.	Student has mastered all the skills/ knowledge for this unit and works well independently doing higher level alternate learning activities.

Date _____

Test score _____ Checklist Indicator(s) _____

Observation(s)

Performance Assessment
Below Expectation...Exceeds Expectations

Student has an understanding of some of the skills/ knowledge and could compact out of some of the work.	Student has an understanding of almost all of the skills/ knowledge and could usually compact out and do alternate activities.	Student has an understanding of all the skills/knowledge for this unit and could compact out of the entire unit and do alternate activities.	Student has mastered all the skills/ knowledge for this unit but has problems working independently doing higher level alternate activities.	Student has mastered all the skills/ knowledge for this unit and works well independently doing higher level alternate learning activities.

Summarize the Student's Response to Curriculum Compacting

Decision:

☐ Continue curriculum compacting as needed and appropriate

☐ Modify the intervention:

☐ Select / implement a new intervention

☐ Move to the next tier (Tier _____)

☐ Refer for other special services:

Fear of Failure

VIGNETTE: ANTHONY

ANTHONY'S BEHAVIORAL CHARACTERISTICS CHECKLIST

WORST CASE SCENARIO ACTIVITY

FEAR OF FAILURE RTI EXAMPLE

FEAR OF FAILURE RTI FORM

ANTHONY

Anthony is a third grader who always seems to be discouraged. He refuses to take most tests and says, "I'll just fail anyway." His approach to class work is much the same. He is often unwilling to do the work even when it is work he could probably do well. Anthony is not a behavior problem and generally tries to have good behavior in school except for behaviors involving schoolwork. He sits quietly, pays attention, and lines up for PE or to go to the lunchroom. Anthony has a few friends but is shy and reserved in class discussions.

Anthony was one of the students discussed by the school's RTI Problem Solving team at its monthly meeting. The team decided to focus on Anthony's probable fear of failure. One research-based intervention they decided to implement was to give specific praise for effort or any other positive actions. Marzano (2000) identified reinforcing effort and giving praise as one of ten effective research-based instructional strategies. He indicates that praise, when recognizing a student's legitimate achievements, has a positive effect on student achievement.

The other intervention they decided to use with Anthony in a whole class setting was the ***Worst Case Scenario*** activity (see page 31). In this activity, the teacher talks to the class about failure and emphasizes that everyone has gone through times of failure, even people we consider to be great successes. After this, each student writes something he or she would like to do but has never attempted because of a fear of failure. The activity goes through several steps ending with the students realizing that even if the worst possible outcome happens, life still goes on.

Anthony participated in the ***Worst Case Scenario*** activity, but this did not seem to make much difference in his progress. Specific praise over a three-week period did not have a noticeable effect either. However, this may not have been enough time to see any significant results.

When the RTI Problem Solving team met at their next monthly meeting, they decided to continue with specific praise and to target fear of test-taking more specifically.

RTI Behavioral Characteristics Checklist

Directions: *Rate the targeted student using the following indicators.*
You may leave some items blank.

> **W =**   Weak in this area
> **I =**   Improving in this area
> **S =**   Strong in this area

Name of student: _____ Anthony _____

— 1. Has a high, yet realistic self-concept.

— 2. Practices self-discipline and self-control.

W 3. Has a positive attitude about school.

I   4.   Attempts to display appropriate behavior in school.

I   5. Listens to those in authority over him/her.

— 6. Communicates problems and concerns to teachers and others in authority.

W 7. Works to turn failures into successes.

W 8. Can see that failures are opportunities for learning.

— 9. Exhibits flexible thinking about his/her behavior and problems.

— 10. Takes responsibility for problems and does not put all the blame on others.

— 11. Recognizes his/her contribution to negative situations.

— 12. Functions well in a group working on a constructive project.

— 13. Has a close friend(s) with whom he/she shares similar (socially acceptable) interests.

— 14. Has friends who are achievers and have positive attitudes about school.

— 15. Uses influence over others in a positive way.

Specific behaviors can be identified and targeted by using this checklist. You can also identify patterns of positive or negative behaviors.

Worst Case Scenario

Failure!! It's something we'd all like to avoid thinking about, but it's a fact of everyone's life. It may sound strange, but every successful person has been a failure at some point in his or her life. For example, in 2000, our current President Barack Obama lost a Democratic primary where he was running for the U.S. House of Representatives. Even though he failed to win that election, he won other elections and eventually became President. There are kids (and adults, too) who never try to do anything because they are so afraid they might not do it right. They have a **fear of failure**.

A famous scientist and author Dr. Isaac Asimov once said, ***"Some things are worth a reasonable amount of hot water."*** In other words, you are not going to succeed and make everyone happy every time. You might get into "hot water" some of the time. You might make mistakes along the way. That's OK!

Any attempt to do something, even if it doesn't work out the way you'd hoped, is a victory…if you have the self-confidence to make the attempt. If fact, the worst failure in life is not to have tried at all.

Maybe you've thought of some things you'd like to try. Maybe you have some goals you think you can reach someday, but you are really hesitant to work on them. You may think you are not good enough or smart enough or talented enough to do them.

Think About It!

Now think about your fear of failure. What is one thing you would like to do that you have never done? _____

_____

WHAT ARE YOU AFRAID WILL HAPPEN IF YOU TRY IT AND DON'T SUCCEED?

_____

THEN WHAT WOULD HAPPEN?

_____

THEN WHAT WOULD YOU DO?

_____

WHAT IS THE WORST THING THAT COULD HAPPEN?

_____

Coil RTI Progress Monitoring Form™
Fear of Failure

Student's Name Anthony

Targeted Skill, Knowledge, or Behavior
- Overcoming a fear of failure

Pre-assessment: (Record all that apply)

Date(s) of Pre-assessment _____

Test score(s) Refused to take Checklist Indicator(s) RTI Behavioral Characteristics
                                        3, 7 & 8 Weaknesses, 4 & 5 Improving

Observation(s)

Unwilling to do work
Verbalizes "I'll just fail anyway"

Performance Assessment

Below Expectation..Exceeds Expectations

Student considers himself a failure in everything so does not attempt any of the work.	Student recognizes that failure can be a way to learn things and that he has both strengths and weaknesses.	Student recognizes that persistence and effort will help over-come the fear of failure.	Student consistently attempts to beat his/her "personal best."	Student learns from mistakes, recognizes his strengths and weaknesses, and accomplishes both easy and difficult tasks.

Strategies or Interventions: (Describe or list below)

Intervention or Strategy	Person Responsible	Timeline
1. Give specific praise for positive actions.	All adults who work with Anthony Classroom teacher	3 weeks
2. Do "Worst-Case Scenario" activity with whole class to open up discussion on dealing with failure.		2 days
3. Use RTI Behavioral Characteristics Checklist again to monitor strengths and weaknesses.	Guidance counselor	End of week 3

Formative Assessments *(Monitoring the Student's Response to Fear of Failure Interventions)*

Date <u>2 week time span</u>

Test score _____   Checklist Indicator(s) <u>same as above</u>

Observation(s)

Specific praise seems to have little effect.

Performance Assessment

Below Expectation...Exceeds Expectations

Student considers himself a failure in everything so does not attempt any of the work.	Student recognizes that failure can be a way to learn things and that he has both strengths and weaknesses.	Student recognizes that persistence and effort will help overcome the fear of failure.	Student consistently attempts to beat his/her "personal best."	Student learns from mistakes, recognizes his strengths and weaknesses, and accomplishes both easy and difficult tasks.

Date <u>Beginning of week 3</u>

Test score _____   Checklist Indicator(s) _____

Observation(s)

Worst case scenario intervention helped open up a discussion about failure.

Performance Assessment

Below Expectation...Exceeds Expectations

Student considers himself a failure in everything so does not attempt any of the work.	Student recognizes that failure can be a way to learn things and that he has both strengths and weaknesses.	Student recognizes that persistence and effort will help overcome the fear of failure.	Student consistently attempts to beat his/her "personal best."	Student learns from mistakes, recognizes his strengths and weaknesses, and accomplishes both easy and difficult tasks.

Date <u>End of week 3</u>

Test score _____   Checklist Indicator(s) <u>no change in Behavioral Characteristics</u>

Observation(s)

Anthony is still very negative and continues to see himself as a failure. Recognizes that everyone has strengths and that you can learn from failure, but does not apply this to his own life.

Performance Assessment

Below Expectation...Exceeds Expectations

Student considers himself a failure in everything so does not attempt any of the work.	Student recognizes that failure can be a way to learn things and that he has both strengths and weaknesses.	Student recognizes that persistence and effort will help overcome the fear of failure.	Student consistently attempts to beat his/her "personal best."	Student learns from mistakes, recognizes his strengths and weaknesses, and accomplishes both easy and difficult tasks.

Summarize the Student's Response to Fear of Failure Interventions

1. Anthony did not respond to the planned interventions as well as we had hoped. He acknowledged that he had some strengths and that experiencing failure could lead to learning new things, but he still is afraid to be a risk-taker especially when taking tests.

2. Anthony participated in the "Worst Case Scenario" activity and talked about his fear of failure, but this did not have an impact on his actions in school.

3. The RTI Behavioral Characteristics Checklist shows significant weaknesses in having a positive attitude, turning failures into successes, and seeing failures as opportunities for learning.

Decision:

☐ Continue these interventions as needed and appropriate

X Modify the intervention:

    Work more specifically on the fear of taking tests.
    Build on his attempts to display appropriate behavior – continue to give specific praise.

☐ Select / implement a new intervention

☐ Move to the next tier (Tier **2**)

    Work on test-taking skills with tutor or paraprofessional.

☐ Refer for other special services:

Coil RTI Progress Monitoring Form™
Fear of Failure

Student's Name _____

Targeted Skill, Knowledge, or Behavior
- **Overcoming a fear of failure**

Pre-assessment: *(Record all that apply)*

Date(s) of Pre-assessment _____

Test score(s) _____ Checklist Indicator(s) _____

Observation(s) _____

Performance Assessment

Below Expectation..Exceeds Expectations

Student considers himself a failure in everything so does not attempt any of the work.	Student recognizes that failure can be a way to learn things.	Student recognizes that persistence and effort will help overcome the fear of failure.	Student consistently attempts to beat his/her "personal best."	Student learns from mistakes, recognizes his strengths and weaknesses, and accomplishes both easy and difficult tasks.

Strategies or Interventions: *(Describe or list below)*

Formative Assessments *(Monitoring the Student's Response to Fear of Failure Interventions)*

Date _____

Test score _____ Checklist Indicator(s) _____

Observation(s)

Performance Assessment
Below Expectation...Exceeds Expectations

Student considers himself a failure in everything so does not attempt any of the work.	Student recognizes that failure can be a way to learn things.	Student recognizes that persistence and effort will help overcome the fear of failure.	Student consistently attempts to beat his/her "personal best."	Student learns from mistakes, recognizes his strengths and weaknesses, and accomplishes both easy and difficult tasks.

Date _____

Test score _____ Checklist Indicator(s) _____

Observation(s)

Performance Assessment
Below Expectation...Exceeds Expectations

Student considers himself a failure in everything so does not attempt any of the work.	Student recognizes that failure can be a way to learn things.	Student recognizes that persistence and effort will help overcome the fear of failure.	Student consistently attempts to beat his/her "personal best."	Student learns from mistakes, recognizes his strengths and weaknesses, and accomplishes both easy and difficult tasks.

Date _____

Test score _____ Checklist Indicator(s) _____

Observation(s)

Performance Assessment
Below Expectation...Exceeds Expectations

Student considers himself a failure in everything so does not attempt any of the work.	Student recognizes that failure can be a way to learn things.	Student recognizes that persistence and effort will help overcome the fear of failure.	Student consistently attempts to beat his/her "personal best."	Student learns from mistakes, recognizes his strengths and weaknesses, and accomplishes both easy and difficult tasks.

Summarize the Student's Response to Fear of Failure Interventions

Decision:

☐ Continue these interventions as needed and appropriate

☐ Modify the intervention:

☐ Select / implement a new intervention

☐ Move to the next tier (Tier _____)

☐ Refer for other special services:

Goal Setting

VIGNETTE: SHANE

"WHAT CAN YOU LEARN FROM THE WORLD OF SPORTS?"

LIFELINE ACTIVITY

GOAL SETTING RTI EXAMPLE

GOAL SETTING RTI FORM

SHANE

Ten year old Shane is a dreamer but is not much of a goal setter. His conversations are peppered with references to the great things he is going to do in the future, but he never has a plan to work toward any of these things. He says he is going to improve his grades and his schoolwork but this never happens. He claims he is such a good singer that he will win American Idol someday but has no plans for the future if that doesn't happen! Shane needs some specific interventions to teach him how to work on both short-term and long-term goals.

An effective research-based intervention (Marzano 2003) is setting goals and objectives for students and providing feedback as they progress. Goal setting is the process of establishing direction and purpose for students. Providing frequent and specific feedback related to learning goals is one of the most effective strategies to increase student achievement.

Shane knew little about how to set goals, see progress toward goals, or assess himself at the end of the intervention. At the beginning of the monitoring process he could set no realistic short- or long-term goals. He was unable to complete either goal setting form (see pages 175, 176).

One intervention we tried with Shane was the *"What Can You Learn from the World of Sports"* activity (see page 40). Many ideas and concepts present in sports involve goal setting. The purpose of this activity is to connect these ideas to success in school and success in the future. There are fifteen ideas listed in this activity. When using it with students, find out which of these ideas resonate with them and then make connections to goal setting in other parts of life. I have found that these concepts work well with any sport and also with video games. There are many connections with learning to play a musical instrument for students who are more musically inclined.

This activity works well as a Tier 1 (whole class) intervention or Tier 2 (small group) intervention. Sometimes I go over all 15 ideas while at other times I take them one at a time and use them as the *Idea of the Week* for discussion and journal writing.

After monitoring Shane's progress for three weeks we are ready to try another intervention – the Lifeline Activity (see page 41). Goal setting is an ongoing process throughout life. Having students learn this process as they focus directly on specific academic goals is important. Equally significant is having them learn to set and keep track of their progress, both behavioral and academic goals, in all aspects of their life.

What Can You Learn from the World of Sports?

Below are 15 sports ideas to encourage top perfor mance. They are also very useful concepts for other parts of life. Write your ideas about how these could apply to your life in school or at home. Discuss with a friend, your parents, or another adult.

1. Show up both for practice and for the main event.

2. Practice skills before the big performance.

3. Know where you're heading and know what the goal is.

4. Have several game plans, not just one.

5. Don't count on the one thing that is the least likely to occur.

6. Work toward small goals (short-term goals) to reach larger goals.

7. Don't give up because you get a penalty or make a mistake.

8. Figure out what you want to accomplish and then plan backwards.

9. Have a coach and have people who cheer you on.

10. Know the rules and abide by them.

11. Have the right equipment and know how to use it.

12. Listen to the referee.

13. Work as a team to get things done.

14. Strive to beat your personal best.

15. You don't need to win every time to be a big success.

from Becoming An Achiever. Carolyn Coil. Pieces of Learning. www.piecesoflearning.com

Lifeline Activity

This intervention can be done for a whole class, in a small group, or individually. It is a hands-on activity, the purpose of which is to show students that what they have done in the past is connected to their lives in the present and can point the way to future goals.

Materials:

Three sets of index cards (approximately five cards in each set) in three different colors for each student who is doing the activity

Procedure:

Distribute the sets of index cards to each student. One color will be used for past events and people, a second color for present day activities and people, and a third color for hopes and dreams for the future. Tell the students to begin with the past and write one significant thing on each card. Then do the same for the present and future.

After the three sets of lifeline cards are completed, each student will sort his or her cards in a number of ways to identify connections, look at challenges, and see patterns from the past and present that can give clues to future actions. After examining all the cards students will:

- See gaps that can become short-term goals
- Decide which goals make the most sense to start working on
- Write other goals for the future not included on the index cards

This activity encourages students to examine their lives and see realistic pathways to working on both short-term and long-term goals.

Coil RTI Progress Monitoring Form™
Goal Setting

Student's Name ___Shane_____

Targeted Skill, Knowledge, or Behavior
- Setting short-term and long-term goals

Pre-assessment: (Record all that apply)

Date(s) of Pre-assessment _____

Test score(s) _____ Checklist Indicator(s) Goal setting forms pgs. _____

Observation(s)

Student could not complete either goal setting form. Sets few if any goals.

Performance Assessment

Below Expectation...Exceeds Expectations

Student does not have any realistic short- or long-term goals.	Student sets minimal short-term goals in one area of his/her life.	Student sets both long- and short-term goals for his/her academic and personal life.	Student has a plan for meeting at least some of his/her goals and checks progress often.	Student has a plan for meeting a number of short- and long-term goals, monitors progress and plans backwards to accomplish them.

Strategies or Interventions: (Describe or list below)

Intervention or Strategy	Person Responsible	Timeline
1. Do "What Can You Learn From the World of Sports?" activity with whole class discussion.	Classroom teacher	2 weeks
2. Try goal setting forms again.	Classroom teacher	after 3 weeks

Formative Assessments *(Monitoring the Student's Response to Goal Setting Interventions)*

Date ___end of 2 weeks___

Test score _____ Checklist Indicator(s) _____

Observation(s)

Student contributed to class discussion on sports analogies over a two week period. Was then able to write some short-term goals.

Performance Assessment

Below Expectation...Exceeds Expectations

Student does not have any realistic short- or long-term goals.	Student sets minimal short-term goals in one area of his/her life.	Student sets both long- and short-term goals for his/her academic and personal life.	Student has a plan for meeting at least some of his/her goals and checks progress often.	Student has a plan for meeting a number of short- and long-term goals, monitors progress and plans backwards to accomplish them.

Date ___beginning of week 3___

Test score _____ Checklist Indicator(s) <u>Goal setting form pg.   – left column</u>

Observation(s)

Goals are unrealistic, but student is beginning to understand the process of goal setting.

Performance Assessment

Below Expectation...Exceeds Expectations

Student does not have any realistic short- or long-term goals.	Student sets minimal short-term goals in one area of his/her life.	Student sets both long- and short-term goals for his/her academic and personal life.	Student has a plan for meeting at least some of his/her goals and checks progress often.	Student has a plan for meeting a number of short- and long-term goals, monitors progress and plans backwards to accomplish them.

Date ___end of week 3___

Test score _____ Checklist Indicator(s) <u>Goal setting form pg.   – goal and 3 steps</u>

Observation(s)

Needs more work and practice on how to plan and reach goals.

Performance Assessment

Below Expectation...Exceeds Expectations

Student does not have any realistic short- or long-term goals.	Student sets minimal short-term goals in one area of his/her life.	Student sets both long- and short-term goals for his/her academic and personal life.	Student has a plan for meeting at least some of his/her goals and checks progress often.	Student has a plan for meeting a number of short- and long-term goals, monitors progress and plans backwards to accomplish them.

Summarize the Student's Response to Goal Setting Interventions

1. Student began the process of planning for short-, medium-, and long-term goals.

2. Was able to do goal setting more successfully after the whole class discussion of the relationship between sports and goals.

3. He needs to work on having a plan for implementing his goals.

Decision:

X   Continue these interventions as needed and appropriate

     Do Lifeline Activity (pg._____), then reassess using Goal Setting form on pg. _____.

☐ Modify the intervention:

☐ Select / implement a new intervention

☐ Move to the next tier (Tier _____)

☐ Refer for other special services:

Coil RTI Progress Monitoring Form™
Goal Setting

Student's Name _____

Targeted Skill, Knowledge, or Behavior
- **Setting short-term and long-term goals**

Pre-assessment: *(Record all that apply)*

Date(s) of Pre-assessment _____

Test score(s) _____ Checklist Indicator(s) _____

Observation(s)

Performance Assessment

Below Expectation...Exceeds Expectations

Student does not have any realistic short- or long-term goals.	Student sets minimal short-term goals in one area of his/her life.	Student sets both long- and short-term goals for his/her academic and personal life.	Student has a plan for meeting at least some of his/her goals and checks progress often.	Student has a plan for meeting a number of short- and long-term goals, monitors progress and plans backwards to accomplish them.

Strategies or Interventions: *(Describe or list below)*

Intervention or Strategy   **Person Responsible**   **Timeline**

Formative Assessments *(Monitoring the Student's Response to Goal Setting Interventions)*

Date _____

Test score _____ Checklist Indicator(s) _____

Observation(s)

Performance Assessment
Below Expectation..Exceeds Expectations

Student does not have any realistic short- or long-term goals.	Student sets minimal short-term goals in one area of his/her life.	Student sets both long- and short-term goals for his/her academic and personal life.	Student has a plan for meeting at least some of his/her goals and checks progress often.	Student has a plan for meeting a number of short- and long-term goals, monitors progress and plans backwards to accomplish them.

Date _____

Test score _____ Checklist Indicator(s) _____

Observation(s)

Performance Assessment
Below Expectation..Exceeds Expectations

Student does not have any realistic short- or long-term goals.	Student sets minimal short-term goals in one area of his/her life.	Student sets both long- and short-term goals for his/her academic and personal life.	Student has a plan for meeting at least some of his/her goals and checks progress often.	Student has a plan for meeting a number of short- and long-term goals, monitors progress and plans backwards to accomplish them.

Date _____

Test score _____ Checklist Indicator(s) _____

Observation(s)

Performance Assessment
Below Expectation..Exceeds Expectations

Student does not have any realistic short- or long-term goals.	Student sets minimal short-term goals in one area of his/her life.	Student sets both long- and short-term goals for his/her academic and personal life.	Student has a plan for meeting at least some of his/her goals and checks progress often.	Student has a plan for meeting a number of short- and long-term goals, monitors progress and plans backwards to accomplish them.

Summarize the Student's Response to Goal Setting Interventions

Decision:

☐ Continue these interventions as needed and appropriate

☐ Modify the intervention:

☐ Select / implement a new intervention

☐ Move to the next tier (Tier _____)

☐ Refer for other special services:

Graphic Organizers

Vignette: Sophia

Graphic Organizers RTI example

Graphic Organizers RTI form

SOPHIA

Sophia has difficulty learning new concepts, new information, and new vocabulary. This is particularly evident in science and social studies where much of the content is information she has not heard before. Her background knowledge is weak compared with others in the class. At times she seems confused and cannot connect what she already knows to the new facts, ideas, and words she is learning. Although Sophia's knowledge base is less extensive than others and she appears to take longer to catch on to new information, given a bit more time and some targeted interventions she should be able to succeed in school.

Knowledge is both linguistic and visual. To assist students in learning one, it is often good to teach using the other. Visual instructional techniques such as graphic organizers, charts, graphs, pictures, diagrams, models, drawings, etc. improve learning and make abstract concepts more concrete. A number of successful research-based instructional strategies involve visual images and graphic representations (Leddick, 2005).

Sophia is a child who lives in poverty. Her experiences are not as rich, nor her vocabulary as developed, as some of the other students in her class. She has less in her realm of experiences to connect to the new information and concepts she is learning. Using graphic organizers is an excellent intervention to show her in a concrete way what she already knows and to connect that knowledge to new concepts and ideas. The visual aspect of this strategy clarifies the connections in a way that only words do not.

Graphic and visual organizers vary greatly in type and design. Some can be complex such as a lengthy diagram that shows an involved scientific concept or a graph depicting several sets of data. On the other hand, graphic organizers and other visuals can include simple charts, concept maps with just a few extensions, line drawings, two- or three-step diagrams, and storyboards. In addition, visuals can be computer-generated or drawn by hand. All of this provides motivation and understanding for the struggling student.

For examples of graphic organizers to use with your students, see pages 177-179.

Coil RTI Progress Monitoring Form™
Using Graphic Organizers

Student's Name _____Sophia_____

Targeted Skill, Knowledge, or Behavior
- Organizing facts and information visually
- Understanding how to use a variety of graphic organizers

Pre-assessment: (Record all that apply)

Date(s) of Pre-assessment _____

Test score(s) 40%-50% Checklist Indicator(s) _____

Observation(s)

Sophia has trouble with academic vocabulary, concept development, identification of people and places, and seeing connections between what she already knows and what she needs to learn. She has difficulty understanding how to use graphic organizers to help her learn these things.

Performance Assessment

Below Expectation..Exceeds Expectations

Does not understand how to use a graphic organizer.	Writes the main idea or concept in a graphic organizer.	Writes the main idea plus one or two details in a graphic organizer.	Writes the main idea and several details in more than one type of graphic organizer.	Writes the main idea, several supporting details plus unique facts or observations in a variety of graphic organizers.

Strategies or Interventions (Describe or list below)

Intervention or Strategy	**Person Responsible**	**Timeline**
Introduce this student to a variety of graphic organizers.	Classroom teacher	Ongoing

- Use Venn Diagrams for concept development in science and social studies.
- Use concept maps and webs as a means of showing visually what the student already knows.
- Use various visual organizers and pictures to increase this student's understanding of academic vocabulary.

Formative Assessments *(Monitoring the Student's Response to Graphic Organizer Interventions)*

Date __After 3 weeks__

Test score __60% on science test__   Checklist Indicator(s) _____

Observation(s)

Science test was mostly academic vocabulary. Used several vocabulary concept maps to learn the vocabulary with one word definition and examples on each map. Also used a graphic organizer for her to write the science ideas she already knew.

Performance Assessment

Below Expectation...Exceeds Expectations

Does not under-stand how to use a graphic organizer.	Writes the main idea or concept in a graphic organizer.	Writes the main idea plus one or two details in a graphic organizer.	Writes the main idea and several details in more than one type of graphic organizer.	Writes the main idea, several supporting details plus unique facts or observations in the graphic organizer.

Date __After 6 weeks__

Test score __60-65% range on a variety of tests and quizzes__ Checklist Indicator(s) _____

Observation(s)

Sophia uses a variety of visual organizers and pictures to learn new concepts and academic vocabulary.

Performance Assessment

Below Expectation...Exceeds Expectations

Does not under-stand how to use the graphic organizer.	Writes the main idea or concept in the graphic organizer.	Writes the main idea plus one or two details in the graphic organizer.	Writes the main idea and several details in **more than one type of graphic organizer.**	Writes the main idea, several supporting details plus unique facts or observations in the graphic organizer.

Date __After 3 months__

Test scores __65-75% range on a variety of tests and quizzes__ Checklist Indicator(s) _____

Observation(s)

Sophia continues to use a variety of graphic organizers. She has difficulty including more than one or two ideas in each. She is weak on analyzing using Venn diagrams.

Performance Assessment

Below Expectation...Exceeds Expectations

Does not under-stand how to use the graphic organizer.	Writes the main idea or concept in the graphic organizer.	Writes the main idea plus one or two details in the graphic organizer.	Writes the main idea and several details in **more than one type of graphic organizer**.	Writes the main idea, several supporting details plus unique facts or observations in the graphic organizer.

Summarize the Student's Response to Graphic Organizer Interventions

1. Sophia's knowledge and ability to retain content and learn new vocabulary has increased during the time she has used visual organizers regularly.

2. Sophia's test and quiz scores average 15-25 points higher as compared to the beginning of the intervention process.

3. This student continues to have difficulty comparing, contrasting, and analyzing. This difficulty is evidenced in all content areas and is the biggest factor to explain why her test scores are not higher.

Decision:

X Continue these interventions as needed and appropriate

   Sophia should continue to use a variety of graphic organizers for note-taking, studying, and learning new vocabulary and other subject matter.

X Modify the intervention:

   Emphasize the use of Venn diagrams, T-charts, and other graphic organizers that visually show comparing, contrasting, and analyzing.

☐ Select / implement a new intervention

☐ Move to the next tier (Tier _____)

☐ Refer for other special services:

Coil RTI Progress Monitoring Form™
Using Graphic Organizers

Student's Name _____

Targeted Skill, Knowledge, or Behavior
- **Organizing facts and information visually**
- **Understanding how to use a variety of graphic organizers**

Pre-assessment: *(Record all that apply)*

Date(s) of Pre-assessment _____

Test score(s) _____ Checklist Indicator(s) _____

Observation(s) _____

Performance Assessment

Below Expectation...Exceeds Expectations

Does not under-stand how to use a graphic organizer.	Writes the main idea or concept in a graphic organizer.	Writes the main idea plus one or two details in a graphic organizer.	Writes the main idea and several details in more than one type of graphic organizer.	Writes the main idea, several supporting details plus unique facts or observations in a variety of graphic organizers.

Strategies or Interventions *(Describe or list below)*

Formative Assessments *(Monitoring the Student's Response to Graphic Organizer Interventions)*

Date _____

Test score _____   Checklist Indicator(s) _____

Observation(s)

Performance Assessment

Below Expectation..Exceeds Expectations

Does not under-stand how to use a graphic organizer.	Writes the main idea or concept in a graphic organizer.	Writes the main idea plus one or two details in a graphic organizer.	Writes the main idea and several details in more than one type of graphic organizer.	Writes the main idea, several supporting details plus unique facts or ob-servations in the graphic organizer.

Date _____

Test score _____   Checklist Indicator(s) _____

Observation(s)

Performance Assessment

Below Expectation..Exceeds Expectations

Does not under-stand how to use the graphic organizer.	Writes the main idea or concept in the graphic orga-nizer.	Writes the main idea plus one or two details in the graphic organizer.	Writes the main idea and several details in more than one type of graphic organizer.	Writes the main idea, several sup-porting details plus unique facts or ob-servations in the graphic organizer.

Date _____

Test score _____   Checklist Indicator(s) _____

Observation(s)

Performance Assessment

Below Expectation..Exceeds Expectations

Does not under-stand how to use the graphic organizer.	Writes the main idea or concept in the graphic organizer.	Writes the main idea plus one or two details in the graphic organizer.	Writes the main idea and several details in more than one type of graphic organizer.	Writes the main idea, several sup-porting details plus unique facts or ob-servations in the graphic organizer.

Summarize the Student's Response to Graphic Organizer Interventions

Decision:

☐ Continue these interventions as needed and appropriate

☐ Modify the intervention:

☐ Select / implement a new intervention

☐ Move to the next tier (Tier _____)

☐ Refer for other special services:

Group Work

VIGNETTE: ISABELLA

FLEXIBLE GROUPING PATTERNS

LISTENING SKILLS CHECKLIST

GROUP WORK RTI EXAMPLE

GROUP WORK RTI FORM

ISABELLA

Isabella is popular with her classmates and is very social. She loves to talk and sometimes gets in trouble for talking too much. She has problems focusing in groups. When she is being candid, she admits she considers group work as time to play around and socialize. She sometimes says, "Group work doesn't really count." She probably means she doesn't feel accountable in any way for what goes on in classroom groups and doesn't feel group work is very important.

Isabella's perception of group work is quite similar to the perceptions of many students. They do not consider it to be as important as individual paper/pencil work and definitely not as important as tests. Yet a great deal of research has been done regarding working in groups and teams as a premier 21st century skill.

Stefan Wuchty, Benjamin F. Jones and Brian Uzzi from Northwestern University in Evanston, IL write:

We have used 19.9 million papers over 5 decades and 2.1 million patents to demonstrate that teams increasingly dominate solo authors in the production of knowledge. Research is increasingly done in teams across nearly all fields. Teams typically produce more frequently cited research than individuals do, and this advantage has been increasing over time. Teams now also produce the exceptionally high-impact research, even where that distinction was once the domain of solo authors. These results are detailed for sciences and engineering, social sciences, arts and humanities, and patents, suggesting that the process of knowledge creation has fundamentally changed. (Science 18 May 2007: Vol. 316. no. 5827, pp. 1036 – 1039)

This is but one of many research studies that emphasize the importance of working in groups. Learning this skill, therefore, is of utmost importance for our students. Students struggle with group work for a number of reasons. Some are competitive and don't want to share their work or knowledge. Sometimes group members are mismatched, and one or two students end up doing all the work. Sometimes students are grouped with their friends and want to socialize.

The key to facilitating productive group work in the classroom is knowing which type of grouping is the most appropriate for which learning outcomes and then grouping your students accordingly. Students must understand the expectations for group work and must be taught group work skills. Group work should be monitored regularly in order for students to understand its importance.

Isabella needed RTI progress monitoring in order to focus on and improve her group work skills. The monitoring process was focused and targeted to improve the many group work skills she did not possess. In Isabella's case, the monitoring itself served as an incentive and motivator for her to pay more attention to what she was accomplishing in groups.

Flexible Grouping Patterns for
The Differentiated Classroom

Homogeneous/Ability/Cluster Grouping
- Clusters students of similar ability, readiness, learning style, or interest.
- Usually based on some type of pre-assessment such as prior school performance, teacher observation, or standardized test scores.
- Use for remediation, acceleration, and enrichment.
- Can be used in multi-grade classes.
- Even in a theoretically more homogeneous class, such as an AP class, there are differing ability levels, and sub-grouping may be needed.
- Possible disadvantage: Inflexibility with unchanging groups that don't meet student needs.

Heterogeneous Grouping
- Groups students of differing abilities, levels, or interests.
- Use to help students understand different points of view.
- Works best when reading level or math proficiency is not involved.
- Good for group projects promoting creativity.
- Teaches skills in delegation, leadership, and sharing.
- Possible disadvantage: One or two students do all the work yet everyone in the group gets the same grade.

Individualized Instruction/Independent Study
- Facilitates the management of many achievement levels.
- Self-paced learning at each student's performance level.
- Good in exploring individual interest areas.
- Teaches independent learning, organizational skills, time management, and the development of individual responsibility.
- Must be monitored and appropriately evaluated.
- Possible disadvantage: Too much time without interaction and learning from others.

Whole Class Instruction
- Efficient and effective when presenting new content to all.
- Use for initial instruction, AV presentations, and some enrichment activities.
- Needed when doing a highly motivational activity that should include all students.
- Use for guest speakers, classroom celebrations, and your favorite lecture topics.
- Possible disadvantage: Overuse!!

Pairs/Partners
- Can be based on ability, skill, or interest.
- Works well with both homogeneous and heterogeneous pairs.
- Assures that a student isn't going to get "lost" or not participate in the group setting.
- More focused learning than in a larger grouping.
- Possible disadvantage: Mismatched peer tutors.

These groups should be thought
of as flexible, not permanent

Listening Skills for Group Work Checklist

Student's Name _____Isabella_____

Directions:

*Mark **YES** or **NO** for each item. Items marked **NO** are those the student needs to work on.*

No 1.   Student listens quietly while other group members are talking.

No 2.   Student avoids carrying on side conversations while the group is meeting.

No 3.   Student monitors the noise level of his/her group and the class as a whole and tells the teacher if the noise gets too loud.

No 4.   Student adds his/her own ideas to what others have said.

No 5.   Student asks for clarification when he/she doesn't understand another person's ideas.

No 6.   Student accepts the ideas of others even when he disagrees.

No 7.   Student concentrates on what other people in the group are saying.

No 8.   Student does not interrupt while someone else is talking.

No 9.   Student can summarize the main points of content and knowledge in a group discussion and asks if this is correct.

No 10. Student can summarize what the group has done and said at the end of the group session.

Coil RTI Progress Monitoring Form™
Group Work

Student's Name __Isabella_____

Targeted Skill, Knowledge, or Behavior
- Learning to work productively in a variety of groups

Pre-assessment: *(Record all that apply)*

Date(s) of Pre-assessment _____

Test score(s) _____ Checklist Indicator(s) Listening Skills for Group Work – 'NO' for all items 1-10

Observation(s)

Isabella has problems focusing in groups. Often wastes time and talks about things not on the group work topic or talks to other students not in her group. She is unable to summarize the main points at the end of a group session.

Performance Assessment

Below Expectation..Exceeds Expectations

Student is unable to work in any type of a group. Is disruptive and/or does not participate.	Student is able to work productively with a carefully selected partner.	Student can work productively in either a heterogeneous or homogeneous group but not both.	Student can work productively in both a heterogeneous or homogeneous group.	Student participates fully and sometimes assumes the leadership in any group he or she participates in.

Strategies or Interventions: *(Describe or list below)*

Intervention or Strategy	Person Responsible	Timeline
1. Lessons on Listening Skills in Groups taught to whole class	Classroom teacher	2 weeks
2. Do group work in partners. Monitor using Individual Learning Log.	Classroom teacher	2 weeks
3. Group work in groups of 4-5	Classroom teacher	ongoing

Formative Assessments *(Monitoring the Student's Response to Group Work Intervention)*

Date <u>after 2 weeks</u>

Test score _____   Checklist Indicator(s) <u>With partner – 'YES' for # 1, 2, 4, 7 & 8</u>

Observation(s)

Student participated in class discussion on listening skills. These are much improved. Worked well with partner as evidenced by Checklist and Individual Learning Log.

Performance Assessment

Below Expectation...Exceeds Expectations

Student is unable to work in any type of a group. Is disruptive and/or does not participate.	Student is able to work productively with a carefully selected partner.	Student can work productively in either a heterogeneous or homogeneous group but not both.	Student can work productively in both a heterogeneous or homogeneous group.	Student participates fully and sometimes assumes the leadership in any group he or she participates in.

Date <u>after 3 weeks</u>

Test score _____   Checklist Indicator(s) <u>With group – 'YES' for # 1, 2, 4, 5, 7 & 10</u>

Observation(s)

As evidenced by checklist and Individual Learning Log, this student worked productively in a heterogeneous group for 15-20 minutes each day during week 2.

Performance Assessment

Below Expectation...Exceeds Expectations

Student is unable to work in any type of a group. Is disruptive and/or does not participate.	Student is able to work productively with a carefully selected partner.	Student can work productively in either a heterogeneous or homogeneous group but not both.	Student can work productively in both a heterogeneous or homogeneous group.	Student participates fully and sometimes assumes the leadership in any group he or she participates in.

Date <u>after 4 weeks</u>

Test score _____   Checklist Indicator(s) <u>With a variety of groups – 'YES' for # 1, 2, 4, 5, 7, 8 & 10</u>

Observation(s)

Isabella needs frequent monitoring through the Individual Learning Log and needs reminders to follow Checklist guidelines. With reminders and monitoring, she is working well in groups.

Performance Assessment

Below Expectation...Exceeds Expectations

Student is unable to work in any type of a group. Is disruptive and/or does not participate.	Student is able to work productively with a carefully selected partner.	Student can work productively in either a heterogeneous or homogeneous group but not both.	Student can work productively in both a heterogeneous or homogeneous group.	Student participates fully and sometimes assumes the leadership in any group he or she participates in.

Summarize the Student's Response to Group Work Interventions

1. Writing her Individual Learning Log helped keep Isabella focused on the work of the group rather than seeing group work time as a social event.

2. Listening Skills Group Work Checklist provided a focus on a set of goals to be attained during the group work process.

3. After one month of interventions, Isabella's main weaknesses in group work are accepting the ideas of others when she disagrees with them and being able to summarize the main points of the content and knowledge the group has worked on. (Checklist # 6 & 9)

Decision:

☐ Continue these interventions as needed and appropriate

X Modify the intervention:
Continue Individual Learning Log and add a section asking for a summary of the content and knowledge.

☐ Select / implement a new intervention

☐ Move to the next tier (Tier _____)

☐ Refer for other special services:

Coil RTI Progress Monitoring Form™
Group Work

Student's Name _____

Targeted Skill, Knowledge, or Behavior
- **Learning to work productively in a variety of groups**

Pre-assessment: *(Record all that apply)*

Date(s) of Pre-assessment _____

Test score(s) _____ Checklist Indicator(s) _____

Observation(s)

Performance Assessment
Below Expectation...Exceeds Expectations

Student is unable to work in any type of a group. Is disruptive and/or does not participate.	Student is able to work productively with a carefully selected partner.	Student can work productively in either a heterogeneous or homogeneous group but not both.	Student can work productively in both a heterogeneous or homogeneous group.	Student participates fully and sometimes assumes the leadership in any group he or she participates in.

Strategies or Interventions: *(Describe or list below)*

Formative Assessments *(Monitoring the Student's Response to Group Work Intervention)*

Date _____

Test score _____ Checklist Indicator(s) _____

Observation(s)

Performance Assessment

Below Expectation..Exceeds Expectations

Student is unable to work in any type of a group. Is disruptive and/or does not participate.	Student is able to work productively with a carefully selected partner.	Student can work productively in either a heterogeneous or homogeneous group but not both.	Student can work productively in both a heterogeneous or homogeneous group.	Student participates fully and sometimes assumes the leadership in any group he or she participates in.

Date _____

Test score _____ Checklist Indicator(s) _____

Observation(s)

Performance Assessment

Below Expectation..Exceeds Expectations

Student is unable to work in any type of a group. Is disruptive and/or does not participate.	Student is able to work productively with a carefully selected partner.	Student can work productively in either a heterogeneous or homogeneous group but not both.	Student can work productively in both a heterogeneous or homogeneous group.	Student participates fully and sometimes assumes the leadership in any group he or she participates in.

Date _____

Test score _____ Checklist Indicator(s) _____

Observation(s)

Performance Assessment

Below Expectation..Exceeds Expectations

Student is unable to work in any type of a group. Is disruptive and/or does not participate.	Student is able to work productively with a carefully selected partner.	Student can work productively in either a heterogeneous or homogeneous group but not both.	Student can work productively in both a heterogeneous or homogeneous group.	Student participates fully and sometimes assumes the leadership in any group he or she participates in.

Summarize the Student's Response to Group Work Interventions

Decision:

☐ Continue these interventions as needed and appropriate

☐ Modify the intervention:

☐ Select / implement a new intervention

☐ Move to the next tier (Tier _____)

☐ Refer for other special services:

Learning Preferences

VIGNETTE: MADISON

MADISON'S LEARNING PREFERENCES CHECKLIST

ANIMAL HABITATS ILP™

ANIMAL HABITATS MINI-RUBRIC

LEARNING PREFERENCES RTI EXAMPLE

LEARNING PREFERENCES RTI FORM

MADISON

> *Madison is an average student who often gets in trouble because of her behavior. She is either out of her seat when she shouldn't be, or she is staring out the window and making comments about the animals and trees she sees there. She likes to doodle and responds well to pictures, graphic organizers, and other visuals. Her teacher, Mr. Williams, is familiar with various theories about how students learn and realizes Madison's learning preferences may not be the focus of many classroom activities. At the same time, he is concerned about standardized testing which is basically a paper/pencil activity.*

Learning styles, learning modalities, multiple intelligences, learning profiles, and learning preferences are different terms that basically mean the same thing. All of these indicate that students learn in different ways and have definite strengths and weaknesses depending upon how the content is taught and what learning activities are involved. Research includes that done by Gardner, Dunn & Dunn, Gregorc, Barbe & Swassing, Tomlinson, and many others.

A number of research-based strategies can be used to focus on students' learning preferences. Giving students choices in their learning not only motivates them to learn the standards, knowledge, and skills they need to know but also begins the process of developing autonomous lifelong learners. Giving students choices based on learning preferences has several advantages:

- Students learn good decision-making skills.
- Students learn to take responsibility for their own learning.
- Lessons and activities become more meaningful to students.

Using the **Learning Preferences Checklist**, (page 68) Mr. Williams discovered that Madison's learning preferences are Visual, Kinesthetic, and Naturalist. Choices in activities were delineated using the Individual Lesson Plan™(ILP) format. In this format, student choices are the activities to the left of the dark vertical line. The upper right-hand quadrant of the format indicates the activities required of all students.

Mr. Williams used an ILP™ on Animal Habitats. Madison's Progress Monitoring Form shows success as she works through her two choices of a Visual and a Kinesthetic activity. He used the Animal Habitats Mini-rubric checklist to assess Madison's progress in each activity. Equally important was her success on a traditional pencil/paper test at the end of the unit.

One goal in using Learning Preferences is for students to learn the material in the way most comfortable and understandable for them but then be able to translate that learning to more traditional types of assessments.

Learning Profiles and Preferences Checklist

Write the names of students that come to mind for each of the learning preferences below.

Visual learners: ___Madison_____

- o Learn by seeing, watching demonstrations
- o Enjoy and learn from visual displays and colors
- o Like pictures, graphic organizers, maps, storyboards

Verbal learners: _____

- o Enjoy listening and are always ready to talk
- o Like music, poetry, dialogues, skits, and debates
- o Learn through verbal instructions

Kinesthetic learners: ___Madison_____

- o Learn by hands-on experiences
- o Like working with materials, manipulatives, and tools
- o Remember what they have done more than what they have seen or heard

Technological learners: _____

- o Know how to use technological tools without formal instruction
- o Expertise in using digital cameras, video production tools, smart boards, computer technologies
- o Understand how to integrate various technologies

Musical/Rhythmic learners: _____

- o Have the ability to communicate through music and poetry
- o Can compose and / or perform musically
- o Have a natural rhythm, beat, and harmony

Logical/Mathematical learners: _____

- o Think in a logical, ordered, sequential way
- o Use reasoning and logic to solve problems
- o Use numbers effectively
- o See logical patterns, statements, and relationships

Naturalist learners: ___Madison_____

- o Can create categories and sort / index items accordingly
- o Are able to recognize and make distinctions between things in nature
- o Observe things in nature others would miss

Intrapersonal/Reflective learners: _____

- o Recognize their own strengths and weaknesses
- o Learn from successes and failures
- o Plan for and uses suitable organization and study skills
- o Understand their own hopes, dreams, aspirations, and emotions

Interpersonal / Group Oriented learners: _____

- o Work well as a member of groups
- o Are able to lead and persuade others
- o Respond appropriately to both verbal and non-verbal cues from others
- o Consider advice and opinions of others when making a decision

Individual Lesson Plan™   Animal Habitats

Required Activities Teacher's Choice	Product/Performance Required	Assessment Required Activities
1. Read the chapter in your science book on animal habitats and answer required questions.	1. Answers to questions	1. Accurate answers / Accurate questions
2. Choose one animal. Research information and write a report about this animal and its habitat. Use at least 3 sources	2. Written report	2. Focused on one animal / Has at least 3 sources / Accurate information / Correct written report format
3. Take the final test on animal habitats.	3. Test answers	3. Accuracy of answers / Test score (percentage of correct answers)

Standards/Objectives:
Understand how changes in the environment affect animal habitats.
Identify features of animals that have allowed them to survive changes in the environment.
Gather information from a variety of sources.

Student Choices in Ways to Learn	Product/Performance Student Choice	Due Dates Student Choice Activities
Visual		
Kinesthetic		
Verbal		
Technological		

ACTIVITIES – STUDENT CHOICES

Visual	Verbal
1. Create a poster that persuades others to protect the habitats of wild animals in your area.	5. Write a fiction story from an extinct animal's point of view. Include what happened to the animal's habitat.
2. For one week, graph your observations of birds, squirrels, chipmunks, raccoons or other wild animals in your area. Your graph must have at least 3 animals and three categories.	6. Using the information you researched in Required Activity #1, plan and give a 5 minute oral presentation on an animal and its habitat.

Kinesthetic	Technological
3. Create a song with movements/actions about animal habitats. Make sure you include several facts about habitats in your song.	7. Find three websites that show habitats of endangered species. Type a list of things all three websites agree on and another list of things they disagree about.
4. Design a diorama showing an animal habitat of your choice. Be accurate in showing details of the habitat.	8. Create a slide show of animal habitats near your home. Include at least three animals.

Assessment of Student Choices – Animal Habitats Individual Lesson Plan™

1. Poster (Visual-Verbal)

- Follows Poster criteria card
- Uses persuasive language
- Has good ideas for protecting habitats
- *Extension : Hang posters in at least 10 places around the school or your neighborhood.*

Possible points = _____

2. Graph (Visual-Mathematical)

- Follows Graph criteria card
- Includes at least three wild animals
- Has three different categories for observations
- Includes information for at least one week

Possible points = _____

3. Song (Kinesthetic-Musical)

- Follows Song criteria card
- Includes several facts about animal habitats
- Movements and actions add to the information in the song
- Accurate information

Possible points = _____

4. Diorama (Kinesthetic)

- Follows Diorama criteria card
- Shows a specific animal habitat
- Accurate details
- *Extension: Add written information explaining more about this animal and its habitat.*

Possible points = _____

5. Fiction Story (Verbal)

- Follows Short Story criteria card
- Story is told from an extinct animal's point of view
- Explains what happened to the animal's habitat
- *Extension: Illustrate your story and read to the class.*

Possible points = _____

6. Oral Presentation (Verbal)

- Follows Oral Report criteria card
- Accurate information
- Tells about both the animal and its habitat
- *Extension: Explains differences in information obtained in each of the sources used*

Possible points = _____

7. Lists from Websites (Technological)

- Uses information from 3 websites
- Has a list on things they agree on
- Has a list of things they disagree about
- *Extension: Write an email to the contact at each website explaining the disagreements you found.*

Possible points = _____

8. Slide Show

- Has at least 10 clear slides
- Slides show at least three habitats of three different animals
- Accurate information and pictures
- *Extension: Include words, graphics and/or music in your show.*

Possible points = _____

Coil RTI Progress Monitoring Form™
Learning Preferences

Student's Name _____ Madison _____

Targeted Skill, Knowledge, or Behavior
- Learning preferences: How does this student best learn?

Pre-assessment: (Record all that apply)

Date(s) of Pre-assessment _____

Test score(s) _____ Checklist Indicator(s) Learning preferences:
                                          Naturalist, Visual, Kinesthetic

Observation(s)

Benefits from visual activities and hands-on learning

Performance Assessment

Below Expectation...Exceeds Expectations

Student is rarely given the opportunity to work in his/her favorite learning preference or style and is usually an unsuccessful learner.	Student occasionally works in his/her favorite learning preference or style and learns well that way.	Student often works in his/her favorite learning preference or style and is mostly successful when doing this.	Student always works in his/her favorite learning preference(s) or styles and is usually successful when doing this.	Student is able to work successfully in a variety of learning styles including those less comfortable and more challenging for him/her.

Strategies or Interventions: (Describe or list below)

Identify standards-based activities that target these preferences:
- — Visual
- — Kinesthetic
- — Naturalist

Use Individualized Lesson Plan (ILP)™ format to plan and implement a unit of work. Give the student a choice of learning activities based on learning preference.

Formative Assessments *(Monitoring the Student's Response to Learning Preferences Interventions)*

Date _____

Test score _____ Checklist Indicator(s) <u>Choose a visual and a kinesthetic activity</u>

Observation(s)

Used ILP™ unit on Animal Habitats with student choices

Motivated and focused when working on these two activities.

Performance Assessment

Below Expectation...Exceeds Expectations

| Student is rarely given the opportunity to work in his/her favorite learning preference or style and is usually an unsuccessful learner. | Student occasionally works in his/her favorite learning preference or style and learns well that way. | Student often works in his/her learning preference or style and is mostly successful when doing this. | Student always works in his/her favorite learning preference(s) or styles and is usually successful when doing this. | Student is able to work successfully in a variety of learning styles including those less comfortable and more challenging for him/her. |

Date _____

Test score _____ Checklist Indicator(s) _____

Observation(s)

One activity completed (Visual - #1)

Second activity partially done (Kinesthetic - #4)

Performance Assessment

Below Expectation...Exceeds Expectations

| Student is rarely given the opportunity to work in his/her favorite learning preference or style and is usually an unsuccessful learner. | Student occasionally works in his/her favorite learning preference or style and learns well that way. | Student often works in his/her favorite learning preference or style and is mostly successful when doing this. | Student always works in his/her favorite learning preference(s) or styles and is usually successful when doing this. | Student is able to work successfully in a variety of learning styles including those less comfortable and more challenging for him/her. |

Date _____

Test score <u>85%</u> Checklist Indicator(s) <u>Mini-rubrics for project</u>

Unit test

Observation(s)

Both activities successfully completed.

Test was <u>not</u> in student's preferred style but student scored well.

Performance Assessment

Below Expectation...Exceeds Expectations

| Student is rarely given the opportunity to work in his/her favorite learning preference or style and is usually an unsuccessful learner. | Student occasionally works in his/her favorite learning preference or style and learns well that way. | Student often works in his/her favorite learning preference or style and is mostly successful when doing this. | Student always works in his/her favorite learning preference(s) or styles and is usually successful when doing this. | Student is able to work successfully in a variety of learning styles including those less comfortable and more challenging for him/her. |

Summarize the Student's Response to Learning Preferences Interventions

1. Student was motivated to work on activities in her areas of learning preference.

2. Student also was able to take a traditional test and score 85%. This was not in her learning preference, but she was successful.

3. Learning through different modalities translated into more traditional assessment.

Decision:

X   Continue these interventions as needed and appropriate

   Use student choice activities when possible. Use both the ILP™ and the Tic-Tac-Toe formats.

☐ Modify the intervention:

☐ Select / implement a new intervention

☐ Move to the next tier (Tier _____)

☐ Refer for other special services:

Coil RTI Progress Monitoring Form™
Learning Preferences

Student's Name _____

Targeted Skill, Knowledge, or Behavior
- **Learning preferences: How does this student best learn?**

Pre-assessment: *(Record all that apply)*

Date(s) of Pre-assessment _____

Test score(s) _____ Checklist Indicator(s) _____

Observation(s)

[ ]

Performance Assessment

Below Expectation...Exceeds Expectations

Student is rarely given the opportunity to work in his/her favorite learning preference or style and is usually an unsuccessful learner.	Student occasionally works in his/her favorite learning preference or style and learns well that way.	Student often works in his/her favorite learning preference or style and is mostly successful when doing this.	Student always works in his/her favorite learning preference(s) or styles and is usually successful when doing this.	Student is able to work successfully in a variety of learning styles including those less comfortable and more challenging for him/her.

Strategies or Interventions: *(Describe or list below)*

Formative Assessments *(Monitoring the Student's Response to Learning Preferences Interventions)*

Date _____

Test score _____ Checklist Indicator(s) _____

Observation(s)

Performance Assessment

Below Expectation...Exceeds Expectations

Student is rarely given the opportunity to work in his/her favorite learning preference or style and is usually an unsuccessful learner.	Student occasionally works in his/her favorite learning preference or style and learns well that way.	Student often works in his/her favorite learning preference or style and is mostly successful when doing this.	Student always works in his/her favorite learning preference(s) or styles and is usually successful when doing this.	Student is able to work successfully in a variety of learning styles including those less comfortable and more challenging for him/her.

Date _____

Test score _____ Checklist Indicator(s) _____

Observation(s)

Performance Assessment

Below Expectation...Exceeds Expectations

Student is rarely given the opportunity to work in his/her favorite learning preference or style and is usually an unsuccessful learner.	Student occasionally works in his/her favorite learning preference or style and learns well that way.	Student often works in his/her favorite learning preference or style and is mostly successful when doing this.	Student always works in his/her favorite learning preference(s) or styles and is usually successful when doing this.	Student is able to work successfully in a variety of learning styles including those less comfortable and more challenging for him/her.

Date _____

Test score _____ Checklist Indicator(s) _____

Observation(s)

Performance Assessment

Below Expectation...Exceeds Expectations

Student is rarely given the opportunity to work in his/her favorite learning preference or style and is usually an unsuccessful learner.	Student occasionally works in his/her favorite learning preference or style and learns well that way.	Student often works in his/her favorite learning preference or style and is mostly successful when doing this.	Student always works in his/her favorite learning preference(s) or styles and is usually successful when doing this.	Student is able to work successfully in a variety of learning styles including those less comfortable and more challenging for him/her.

Summarize the Student's Response to Learning Preferences Interventions

Decision:

☐ Continue these interventions as needed and appropriate

☐ Modify the intervention:

☐ Select / implement a new intervention

☐ Move to the next tier (Tier _____)

☐ Refer for other special services:

Negative Peer Pressure

VIGNETTE: MELINDA

MELINDA'S BEHAVIORAL CHARACTERISTICS CHECKLIST

NEGATIVE PEER PRESSURE RTI EXAMPLE

NEGATIVE PEER PRESSURE RTI FORM

MELINDA

Melinda is a middle school student who is highly influenced by a "wrong crowd" of four other girls. When she is not with them, Melinda works well in school. However, their opinions are leading her to have poor work habits and a negative attitude about school. These girls are not achievers and have convinced Melinda that it is "not cool" to get good grades or achieve in school. This attitude is reflected in her test scores which have dropped significantly over the past three months. They currently average between 50%-70%. Melinda was identified as a gifted student in second grade, and her academic history during previous school years shows that she is capable of doing much better than she is at the present time.

Melinda's teachers are very concerned that she not continue in this downward academic spiral. Being influenced by negative peer pressure is fairly common during the middle school years, so they wanted to reverse it as quickly as possible.

One research-based strategy they decided to try was bibliotherapy. The Language Arts teacher said that one of the Literature Circle groups could read a story focusing on positive friendships. Melinda was assigned to that group. The school guidance counselor then could use a discussion of the book with Melinda and a few other students to delve into the issues of friendships and the negative influence some friends could have.

Another intervention they decided to try was to match Melinda with a Big Sister. The community coordinator of this program found a Big Sister for Melinda, and this had a very positive effect. Melinda and her Big Sister, a student at a local university, enjoyed being with one another, and the Big Sister became an excellent role model.

Finally, Melinda began studying with three other girls in social studies and science classes. These girls are achievers and have encouraged Melinda to study. Over time they have begun to reverse the influence of Melinda's non-achieving friends.

RTI Behavioral Characteristics Checklist

Directions: *Rate the targeted student using the following indicators.*
               You may leave some items blank.

W =	Weak in this area
I =	Improving in this area
S =	Strong in this area

Name of student: __Melinda__

— 1. Has a high, yet realistic self-concept.

— 2. Practices self-discipline and self control.

W 3. Has a positive attitude about school.

— 4.   Attempts to display appropriate behavior in school.

— 5. Listens to those in authority over him/her.

— 6. Communicates problems and concerns to teachers and others in authority

— 7. Works to turn failures into successes.

— 8. Can see that failures are opportunities for learning.

— 9. Exhibits flexible thinking about his/her behavior and problems.

— 10. Takes responsibility for problems and does not put all the blame on others.

— 11. Recognizes his/her contribution to negative situations.

— 12. Functions well in a group working on a constructive project.

W 13. Has a close friend(s) with whom he/she shares similar (socially acceptable)

        interests.

W 14. Has friends who are achievers and have positive attitudes about school.

W 15. Uses influence over others in a positive way.

Specific behaviors can be identified and targeted by using this checklist. You can also identify patterns of positive or negative behaviors.

Coil RTI Progress Monitoring Form™
Negative Peer Pressure

Student's Name __Melinda__

Targeted Skill, Knowledge, or Behavior
- <u>Resisting negative peer pressure</u>
- <u>Choosing appropriate friends and students with which to work</u>

Pre-assessment: *(Record all that apply)*

Date(s) of Pre-assessment _____

Test score(s) <u>50-70%</u>   Checklist Indicator(s) <u>Behavioral Characteristics: 3, 13, 14, 15</u>
(Range of scores on classroom tests)   <u>weaknesses</u>

Observation(s)

This student is heavily influenced by her friends all of whom do poorly in school.

Performance Assessment

Below Expectation..Exceeds Expectations

Student only has friends who are not achievers, hate school and do no work at home or at school.	Student understands that his friends are not helping him and would like to change.	Student works with an achieving partner of the same ability level and is successful in his work.	Student has friends in school who are achievers and with whom he studies before tests.	Student is able to influence his non-achieving friends to do better in school and exerts positive peer pressure on them.

Strategies or Interventions: *(Describe or list below)*

Intervention or Strategy	Person Responsible	Timeline
1. Pair student with Big Sister	Big Sister Community Coordinator	3 months
2. Bibliotherapy: Use books and stories about positive friendships	Language Arts teacher Guidance counselor	6 weeks
3. Whole class activity about friendships	Classroom Teacher	1-3 days

Formative Assessments *(Monitoring the Student's Response to Negative Peer Pressure Interventions)*

Date <u>after 2 weeks</u>

Test score _____ Checklist Indicator(s) _____

Observation(s)

Two meetings with her Big Sister have been very positive. Melinda's attitude toward school is more positive. Melinda smiles and laughs more than before.

Performance Assessment

Below Expectation ....Exceeds Expectations

| Student only has friends who are not achievers, hate school and do no work at home or at school. | Student understands that his friends are not helping him and would like to change. | Student works with an achieving partner of the same ability level and is successful in his work. | Student has friends in school who are achievers and with whom he studies before tests. | Student is able to influence his non-achieving friends to do better in school and exerts positive peer pressure on them. |

Date <u>after 1 month</u>

Test score(s) <u>80-85%</u> Checklist Indicator(s) <u>Page 17 – Number 15 now a strength</u>
(Range of scores on classroom tests)

Observation(s)

This student has made friends with three other girls who are achievers. They study in class together on a regular basis. Friendship started after whole class discussion about friends and study partners.

Performance Assessment

Below Expectation ....Exceeds Expectations

| Student only has friends who are not achievers, hate school and do no work at home or at school. | Student understands that his friends are not helping him and would like to change. | Student works with an achieving partner of the same ability level and is successful in his work. | Student has friends in school who are achievers and with whom he studies before tests. | Student is able to influence his non-achieving friends to do better in school and exerts positive peer pressure on them. |

Date <u>after 6 weeks</u>

Test score(s) <u>80-85%</u>   Checklist Indicator(s) <u>Page 17 – 8 & 15 are now strengths</u>
(Range of scores on classroom tests)

Observation(s)

Guidance counselor reports that the bibliotherapy sessions have resulted in this student sharing some of her problems about friendships and family life. Others in the group have been supportive. Student speaks highly of her Big Sister.

Performance Assessment

Below ExpectationM ....Exceeds Expectations

| Student only has friends who are not achievers, hate school and do no work at home or at school. | Student understands that his friends are not helping him and would like to change. | Student works with an achieving partner of the same ability level and is successful in his work. | Student has friends in school who are achievers and with whom he studies before tests. | Student is able to influence his non-achieving friends to do better in school and exerts positive peer pressure on them. |

81

Summarize the Student's Response to Negative Peer Pressure Interventions

1. Test scores have improved significantly (from 50-70% to 80-85%).

2. Big sister has been a positive influence. Grades, projects, and test scores are at mastery or above since Big Sister began working with her.

3. Study groups with achieving peers have helped this student study more effectively.

Decision:

X Continue these interventions as needed and appropriate

   Continue relationship with Big Sister, continue study groups with achieving peers.

☐ Modify the intervention:

☐ Select / implement a new intervention

☐ Move to the next tier (Tier _____)

☐ Refer for other special services:

82

Coil RTI Progress Monitoring Form™
Negative Peer Pressure

Student's Name _____

Targeted Skill, Knowledge, or Behavior
- **Resisting negative peer pressure**
- **Choosing appropriate friends and students to work with**

Pre-assessment: *(Record all that apply)*

Date(s) of Pre-assessment _____

Test score(s) _____ Checklist Indicator(s) _____

Observation(s)

| |
| |

Performance Assessment

Below Expectation...Exceeds Expectations

Student only has friends who are not achievers, hate school and do no work at home or at school.	Student understands that his friends are not helping him and would like to change.	Student works with an achieving partner of the same ability level and is success-ful in his work.	Student has friends in school who are achievers and with whom he studies before tests.	Student is able to influence his non-achieving friends to do better in school and exerts positive peer pressure on them.

Strategies or Interventions: *(Describe or list below)*

Formative Assessments *(Monitoring the Student's Response to Negative Peer Pressure Interventions)*

Date _____

Test score _____ Checklist Indicator(s) _____

Observation(s)

Performance Assessment
Below Expectation...Exceeds Expectations

Student only has friends who are not achievers, hate school and do no work at home or at school.	Student understands that his friends are not helping him and would like to change.	Student works with an achieving partner of the same ability level and is successful in his work.	Student has friends in school who are achievers and with whom he studies before tests.	Student is able to influence his non-achieving friends to do better in school and exerts positive peer pressure on them.

Date _____

Test score _____ Checklist Indicator(s) _____

Observation(s)

Performance Assessment
Below Expectation...Exceeds Expectations

Student only has friends who are not achievers, hate school and do no work at home or at school.	Student understands that his friends are not helping him and would like to change.	Student works with an achieving partner of the same ability level and is successful in his work.	Student has friends in school who are achievers and with whom he studies before tests.	Student is able to influence his non-achieving friends to do better in school and exerts positive peer pressure on them.

Date _____

Test score _____ Checklist Indicator(s) _____

Observation(s)

Performance Assessment
Below Expectation...Exceeds Expectations

Student only has friends who are not achievers, hate school and do no work at home or at school.	Student understands that his friends are not helping him and would like to change.	Student works with an achieving partner of the same ability level and is successful in his work.	Student has friends in school who are achievers and with whom he studies before tests.	Student is able to influence his non-achieving friends to do better in school and exerts positive peer pressure on them.

Summarize the Student's Response to Negative Peer Pressure Interventions

Decision:

☐ Continue these interventions as needed and appropriate

☐ Modify the intervention:

☐ Select / implement a new intervention

☐ Move to the next tier (Tier _____)

☐ Refer for other special services:

Number Sense

VIGNETTE: MIA

NUMBER SENSE RTI EXAMPLE

NUMBER SENSE RTI FORM

Mia

Six-year-old Mia knows how to count from one to ten though she sometimes misses the numbers seven or eight. She mixes up many of the numbers between eleven and twenty though she usually mentions them all. She has even less understanding about what numbers actually mean. While most of her classmates identify sets of objects and the number of objects in a group, Mia rarely connects counting out loud with the fact that you can use number words to count, sort, and classify objects. When asked to circle groups of items shown by pictures on a worksheet, Mia was unable to do this correctly.

Mia had a great deal of difficulty understanding that number words actually meant something. The majority of students in her class began the school year already knowing how to put objects into sets of five, and some of them could do ten or fifteen. Because of this, the teacher did not spend much time going over these concepts with the whole class.

In examining Mia's progress using checklists of skills that were recorded on individual running records, it was obvious that she needed more help to understand basic number concepts. The K-2 RTI team brainstormed possible interventions for Mia and the three or four other students who were also struggling with these same concepts.

They decided to use kinesthetic and musical approaches to teach number concepts. Learning centers with many math manipulatives were designed to give this small group of students additional practice in identifying and counting objects in a group. Several center activities targeted objects in groups of five. Some more advanced activities in the learning centers focused on groups of ten or fifteen. All activities were hands-on.

Embedded into the learning center activities were several research-based interventions such as having students compare, contrast, classify, and analyze, and allowing students to learn through nonlinguistic, concrete representations.

Another intervention the team decided upon was to use songs with actions. While the songs were counting songs, the actions had the students pick up objects and put them in various group configurations. Research indicates that having students act out content will increase student achievement. Built into this activity was another research-based strategy of giving praise for added effort. Various teachers, including the music teacher, volunteered to do these action songs with the targeted children for at least 15 minutes three times a week.

Over time, Mia mastered the skill of counting and identifying groups of objects and is currently working on the number concepts of less and more.

Coil RTI Progress Monitoring Form™
Number Sense

Student's Name _____Mia_____

Targeted Skill, Knowledge, or Behavior
- Ordering groups of objects by number
- Understanding more, less, and equal

Pre-assessment: (Record all that apply)

Date(s) of Pre-assessment _____

Test score(s) _____   Checklist Indicator(s) Running Records _____

Does not know groups of 5,10,15

Observation(s)

Student cannot identify groups when given pictures on a worksheet.

Performance Assessment

Below Expectation...Exceeds Expectations

Cannot identify the number of objects in a group (Indicate numbers) 5,10,15	Can identify the number of objects in a group. (Indicate numbers) _____	Can identify equal groups of numbers (Indicate numbers) _____ & _____	Can compare groups of numbers by identifying less or more. (Indicate numbers) _____ & _____	Can identify missing numbers in a sequence when looking at groups of numbers. (Indicate numbers) _____

Strategies or Interventions (Describe or list below)

Intervention or Strategy	Person Responsible	Timeline
1. Use math manipulatives in several learning centers. Target skills in identifying objects in a variety of groups.	Classroom teacher Paraprofessional	6 weeks
2. Kinesthetic songs and actions with numbers. Design songs and actions to target specific number concepts.	Volunteers	15 minutes 3 times per week

Formative Assessments *(Monitoring the Student's Response to Number Sense Interventions)*

Date <u>End of 2 weeks</u>

Test score _____   Checklist Indicator(s) _____<u>Running Records</u>_____

Knows groups of 5

Observation(s)

Can sort various objects into groups of 5 when working in the learning center.
Participates in the music/action activities.

Performance Assessment

Below Expectation...Exceeds Expectations

Cannot identify the number of objects in a group (Indicate numbers) <u>10, 15</u>	Can identify the number of objects in a group. (Indicate numbers) <u>5</u>	Can identify equal groups of numbers (Indicate numbers) <u>5</u> & <u>5</u>	Can compare groups of numbers by identifying less or more. (Indicate numbers) _____ & _____	Can identify missing numbers in a sequence when looking at groups of numbers. (Indicate numbers) _____

Date <u>End of 4 weeks</u>

Test score _____   Checklist Indicator(s) _____<u>Running Records</u>_____

Knows groups of 10

Observation(s)

Student is making progress in learning groups of both 5 & 10. Manipulatives have been a good strategy to use for this skill. Music works as a reinforcer of the skills.

Performance Assessment

Below Expectation...Exceeds Expectations

Cannot identify the number of objects in a group (Indicate numbers) <u>15</u>	Can identify the number of objects in a group. (Indicate numbers) <u>5, 10</u>	Can identify equal groups of numbers (Indicate numbers) <u>5,10</u> & <u>5,10</u>	Can compare groups of numbers by identifying less or more. (Indicate numbers) <u>5</u> & <u>10</u>	Can identify missing numbers in a sequence when looking at groups of numbers. (Indicate numbers) _____

Date <u>End of 6 weeks</u>

Test score <u>80%</u>   Checklist Indicator(s) _____

On groups of 5 & 10

Observation(s)

Working on groups of 15 by learning 5+5+5

Performance Assessment

Below Expectation...Exceeds Expectations

Cannot identify the number of objects in a group (Indicate numbers) _____	Can identify the number of objects in a group. (Indicate numbers) <u>5,10,15</u>	Can identify equal groups of numbers (Indicate numbers) <u>5,10</u> & <u>5,10</u>	Can compare groups of numbers by identifying less or more. (Indicate numbers) <u>5</u> & <u>10,15</u>	Can identify missing numbers in a sequence when looking at groups of numbers. (Indicate numbers) _____

Summarize the Student's Response to Number Sense Interventions

1. Mia worked with a variety of manipulatives in math learning center.

2. She has mastered identification of groups of 5 and 10 objects.

3. She is working on groups of 15 objects.

4. She has mastered concept of less and more in groups of objects (10 or less).

5. Mia's test score and running records indicate progress over a six- week period.

Decision:

X   Continue these interventions as needed and appropriate
   Use math manipulatives to supplement general classroom math instruction
   when Mia doesn't understand the concepts being taught.

☐   Modify the intervention:

X   Select / implement a new intervention
   Work on missing numbers in a sequence.

☐   Move to the next tier (Tier _____)

☐   Refer for other special services:

Coil RTI Progress Monitoring Form™
Number Sense

Student's Name _____

Targeted Skill, Knowledge, or Behavior
- **Ordering groups of objects by number**
- **Understanding more, less and equal**

Pre-assessment: *(Record all that apply)*

Date(s) of Pre-assessment _____

Test score(s) _____   Checklist Indicator(s) _____

Observation(s) _____

Performance Assessment

Below Expectation...Exceeds Expectations

Cannot identify the number of objects in a group (Indicate numbers) _____	Can identify the number of objects in a group. (Indicate numbers) _____	Can identify equal groups of numbers (Indicate numbers) _____ & _____	Can compare groups of numbers by identifying less or more. (Indicate numbers) _____ & _____	Can identify missing numbers in a sequence when looking at groups of numbers. (Indicate numbers) _____

Strategies or Interventions *(Describe or list below)*

Formative Assessments *(Monitoring the Student's Response to Number Sense Interventions)*

Date _____

Test score _____   Checklist Indicator(s) _____

Observation(s)

Performance Assessment
Below Expectation...Exceeds Expectations

Cannot identify the number of objects in a group (Indicate numbers) _____	Can identify the number of objects in a group. (Indicate numbers) _____	Can identify equal groups of numbers (Indicate numbers) _____ & _____	Can compare groups of numbers by identifying less or more. (Indicate numbers) _____ & _____	Can identify missing numbers in a sequence when looking at groups of numbers. (Indicate numbers) _____

Date _____

Test score _____   Checklist Indicator(s) _____

Observation(s)

Performance Assessment
Below Expectation...Exceeds Expectations

Cannot identify the number of objects in a group (Indicate numbers) _____	Can identify the number of objects in a group. (Indicate numbers) _____	Can identify equal groups of numbers (Indicate numbers) _____ & _____	Can compare groups of numbers by identifying less or more. (Indicate numbers) _____ & _____	Can identify missing numbers in a sequence when looking at groups of numbers. (Indicate numbers) _____

Date _____

Test score _____   Checklist Indicator(s) _____

Observation(s)

Performance Assessment
Below Expectation...Exceeds Expectations

Cannot identify the number of objects in a group (Indicate numbers) _____	Can identify the number of objects in a group. (Indicate numbers) _____	Can identify equal groups of numbers (Indicate numbers) _____ & _____	Can compare groups of numbers by identifying less or more. (Indicate numbers) _____ & _____	Can identify missing numbers in a sequence when looking at groups of numbers. (Indicate numbers) _____

Summarize the Student's Response to Number Sense Interventions

Decision:

☐ Continue these interventions as needed and appropriate

☐ Modify the intervention:

☐ Select / implement a new intervention

☐ Move to the next tier (Tier _____)

☐ Refer for other special services:

Organizational Skills

VIGNETTE: JACK

JACK'S RTI ORGANIZATION CHECKLIST

INTERVENTIONS TO HELP DEVELOP ORGANIZATIONAL SKILLS

SCHOOL SUPPLIES CHECKLIST

ORGANIZATIONAL SKILLS RTI EXAMPLE

ORGANIZATIONAL SKILLS RTI FORM

JACK

Jack seems to be completely disorganized! His parents know he could be a good student but not unless he learns how to write down his assignments and bring the correct books and materials home so that he can work on his homework. Sometimes they say to him, "Jack, where is your brain? What were you thinking when you left school with no materials and no agenda book for us to sign?"

Jack's teacher is also frustrated about the fact that he completes so few assignments. The school supplies an agenda book for each student, and this book could be very helpful if Jack would write down assignments and then have his parents sign the book every night as is required.

Organizational skills are necessary skills for success in school and in life. Students who have learning difficulties often have problems with organizational skills. Many gifted and high-ability students think they will do fine even if they are not organized. Over time they do not learn these skills and then discover they need them.

One problem with organizational skills is that they are so varied. Everything from having too much "stuff" and no way to find it, to planning a schedule of activities, to writing down and completing assignments are all aspects of organization.

Planning interventions to help a specific student with organizational skills begins with identifying the skills he or she needs to work on. Use the RTI Organization Checklist (page 96) to identify these skills. Then look at suggestions (pages 97, 98) to see what interventions to try with an individual student. If there are a number of problems, target one or two at a time.

In Jack's case, two organizational skills that were causing problems were writing down and completing assignments and remembering to bring appropriate materials to class. While these were not his only problems with organization, we decided to target these and work on them. Jack's parents wanted to help; therefore they were also involved in implementing the interventions.

Organizational skills often depend on writing down, completing, and turning in homework appropriately. Research indicates that providing students with opportunities to deepen their understanding of content and skills often involves homework and practice. Developing good organizational skills is a cornerstone for success in these areas.

RTI Organization Checklist

Directions: *Mark a check under* **Yes** *or* **No** *to indicate how organized this student is.*

Name of student: ____Jack_____

No   **Yes**

___   ___   1. There are things in his/her locker, backpack, desk, or cubby that haven't been looked at in a month or more.

___   ___   2. At home, she/he has a pile of books, comic books, magazines, or videos that have been recorded that she/he hasn't read or seen yet but is going to do some day.

___   _X_   3. This student never writes down assignments because he/she thinks he/she can remember everything that is important.

___   _X_   4. He/she forgets about long-range assignments until it's too late to do a good job on them.

___   ___   5. This student's parents keep track of his/her schedule of after-school activities, and the student just does whatever they tell him/her to do.

___   _X_   6. Once a week or more, this student leaves at home at least one of the following: materials needed for class, homework, notes that should be signed, agenda books, etc.

___   ___   7. This student has a hard time keeping track of his/her keys, glasses, purse, wallet, jacket, shoes, hat, or other things he/she can't leave home or school without.

___   ___   8. This student has trouble remembering important dates like anniversaries, birthdays, class field trips, test dates, etc.

___   ___   9. When this student starts on an assignment or project, he/she has a hard time completing it because of getting distracted easily.

___   ___   10. This student is very disorganized but is motivated to learn organizational skills.

___   ___   Totals

SCORING

10, 9 or 8	Yes – This student has major problems with organization!
7 or 6	Yes – This student needs to develop additional organizational skills.
5, 4 or 3	Yes – This student has good organizational skills but can still improve.
2, 1 or 0	Yes – This student has excellent organizational skills!

This checklist helps to pinpoint areas where students need assistance in becoming more organized. If you look at the items marked "Yes," you will see which areas are organizational problems for an individual student.

Interventions to Help Develop Organizational Skills

1. For students who are "pack rats," have them go through their desks, lockers, backpacks, etc. on a regular basis. This is best done at least every two weeks. Ask them to sort their papers and other belongings into four piles:
   - ❏ Need within the next 24 hours
   - ❏ Need this week
   - ❏ Need sometime but I don't know when
   - ❏ Don't need (throw away)

   Papers and other belongings in the first two categories are usually not large and are easy to deal with. Those in the third category should be put in a box and thrown away if not used within a month.

2. For students who do not plan well, ask them to make a **To Do List** and then prioritize the items. Categories should include:
   - ❏ Extremely Important
   - ❏ Fairly Important
   - ❏ This can wait; it is not important
   - ❏ This doesn't need to be on my list

   Teach students to do the most important priorities first, and make a plan for them to be completed on time.

3. Brainstorm strategies with students who never write down assignments. They probably don't want to write them down or do them, but they can be taught how to make this a habit. Assignment and agenda notebooks work fine if students use them. But when students don't bother we need to come up with creative solutions. Many students like writing assignments on sticky notes and putting the notes on their books or papers. Others (especially those who are technologically inclined) will send themselves an email or text message with the homework assignment. Still others find a "study buddy" who will call and remind them of the assignments that are due. With this organizational skill, the interventions that are the student's idea will be the ones that are the most effective!

4. For students who forget about long-range assignments (or procrastinate doing them), the assignment needs to be broken into smaller segments with checkpoints along the way. An RTI Monitoring Form could help the teacher and the student keep track of the progress being made when working on a long-term assignment or project.

5. Many students who have problems with organization actually have parents who are overly helpful. When the parents keep track of the schedule and the schoolwork and the notes and the homework it is difficult for the student to develop responsibility in those areas. A number of interventions can be used to make students more responsible. Students should:

   - ❏ Keep track of their own belongings, finding a place at home to put all the things that will be needed in school the next day
   - ❏ Keep a calendar or schedule of important dates and events. This may include an individual calendar and a family calendar.
   - ❏ Have a school supplies checklist for use at home and at school (page 98).

School Supplies Checklist

This intervention is one that should be put into practice individually. However, you may want to have many of your students do it and may work with them at the same time as they develop their checklists.

<u>Procedure</u>

Help the student or students brainstorm a list of materials and supplies they need on a routine basis at school each day and ones they need at home to complete homework and projects. When the list is completed, help them make two lists: ***Supplies Needed at School*** and ***Supplies Needed at Home***. Some of the items will be on both lists while others will just be on one of the two lists.

Type each list (or have the student type them) or have the student write the two lists in checklist form on two sides of a 3"x5" card. Laminate the lists so that one list is on the front and the other is on the back of the same paper. Have the student attach the lists to his or her backpack like a luggage tag is attached to a suitcase. The lists can then be used for easy reference as a reminder of the supplies and materials that should be in the backpack going home or going to school.

Sample School Supplies "Luggage Tag" Checklist

<u>Supplies Needed at Home</u>	<u>Supplies Needed at School</u>
_____ Agenda book to be signed by parent	_____ Agenda book signed by parent
_____ Notebook paper	_____ Pencils
_____ Pencils	_____ Pen
_____ Pen-	_____ All books needed for the day
_____ Textbooks needed for assignments	_____ Paper (different kinds)
_____ Notebook or worksheets as needed	_____ Notebook with completed homework
_____ Computer	_____ Any notes or money needed for school
_____ Calculator	_____ Calculator
_____ Other: _____	_____ Other: _____

Coil RTI Progress Monitoring Form™
Organizational Skills

Student's Name __Jack_____

Targeted Skill, Knowledge, or Behavior
- Organizing time, materials, and events
- Planning and prioritizing assignments, dates, and schedules

---

Pre-assessment: *(Record all that apply)*

Date(s) of Pre-assessment _____

Test score(s) _____Checklist Indicator(s) Organization Checklist: 'Yes' for
Numbers 3, 4, 6

Observations

Jack rarely writes down assignments. He often forgets to bring books, note books, paper, pencils, or other needed items to class. He struggles to complete long-range assignments due to procrastination.

Performance Assessment

Below Expectation...Exceeds Expectations

Demonstrates no skill in organizing materials, time, assignments or events.	Writes down assignments but procrastinates in doing them; often loses or does not have materials.	Completes short-term assignments, has most needed materials but does not plan long-term.	Completes short and long-term assignments in a timely manner; has needed materials and uses time wisely.	Plans schedule to include all priorities, completes all long and short term assignments, has needed materials, and uses time wisely.

Strategies or Interventions *(Describe or list below)*

Intervention or Strategy	**Person Responsible**	**Timeline**
1. Use "TO DO" Mindmap and "Assignments To Do" list. Monitor both to see which works better in helping Jack write down and complete assignments.	Classroom teacher	6 weeks
2. Use a School Supplies Checklist attached to Jack's backpack to check materials needed at school and at home.	Jack and parents	6 weeks

Formative Assessments *(Monitoring the Student's Response to Organizational Skills Interventions)*

Date <u>After 2 weeks</u>

Test score _____   Checklist Indicator(s) _____

Observation(s)

Used the "TO DO" Mindmap for writing down assignments. This has helped Jack write down all major assignments and complete 50% of them over a two week period. Procrastinates therefore does not complete the other 50%.

Performance Assessment

Below Expectation...Exceeds Expectations

Demonstrates no skill in organizing materials, time, assignments or events.	Writes down assignments but procrastinates in doing them; often loses or does not have materials.	Completes short-term assignments, has most needed materials but does not plan long-term.	Completes short and long-term assignments in a timely manner; has needed materials and uses time wisely.	Plans schedule to include all priorities, completes all long and short term assignments, has needed materials, and uses time wisely.

Date <u>After 4 weeks</u>

Test score _____   Checklist Indicator(s) _____

Observation(s)

Used the "Assignments To Do" list with less success than the "TO DO" Mindmap. Assignments completed 40% of the time. Brings most materials. Uses School Supplies Checklist regularly. Parents report that Jack is remembering to do this on his own.

Performance Assessment

Below Expectation...Exceeds Expectations

Demonstrates no skill in organizing materials, time, assignments or events.	**Writes down assignments but procrastinates in doing them;** often loses or does not have materials.	**Completes short-term assignments, has most needed materials** but does not plan long-term.	Completes short and long-term assignments in a timely manner; has needed materials and uses time wisely.	Plans schedule to include all priorities, completes all long and short term assignments, has needed materials, and uses time wisely.

Date <u>After 6 weeks</u>

Test score _____   Checklist Indicator(s) _____

Observation(s)

Used the "TO DO" Mindmap to write down assignments. Had a 70% completion rate on short-term assignments. Brings materials to class consistently each day.

Performance Assessment

Below Expectation...Exceeds Expectations

Demonstrates no skill in organizing materials, time, assignments or events.	Writes down assignments but procrastinates in doing them; often loses or does not have materials.	Completes short-term assignments, has most needed materials but does not plan long-term.	Completes short and long-term assignments in a timely manner; has needed materials and uses time wisely.	Plans schedule to include all priorities, completes all long and short term assignments, has needed materials, and uses time wisely.

Summarize the Student's Response to Organizational Skills Interventions

1. Three interventions were tried with this student during a six-week period.

2. The "TO DO" Mindmap was more effective (70% completion of assignments) than the "Assignments To Do" list (40% completion of assignments).

3. School Supplies Checklist attached to this student's backpack worked well in reminding him to bring needed materials to class. This intervention was monitored by Jack's parents who report that by the end of six weeks he is checking the School Supplies Checklist on his own before leaving for school each day.

4. Jack still needs to work on completing short-range assignments and needs to begin an intervention for long-range assignments.

Decision:

X Continue these interventions as needed and appropriate

X Modify the intervention:

   Use an intervention for writing down assignments to focus on long-term assignments of 2 weeks or more.

☐ Select / implement a new intervention

☐ Move to the next tier (Tier _____)

☐ Refer for other special services:

Coil RTI Progress Monitoring Form™
Organizational Skills

Student's Name _____

Targeted Skill, Knowledge, or Behavior
- **Organizing time, materials, and events**
- **Planning and prioritizing assignments, dates, and schedules**

Pre-assessment: *(Record all that apply)*

Date(s) of Pre-assessment _____

Test score(s) _____   Checklist Indicator(s) _____

Observation(s) _____

[   ]

Performance Assessment

Below Expectation..Exceeds Expectations

Demonstrates no skill in organizing materials, time, assignments or events.	Writes down assignments but procrastinates in doing them; often loses or does not have materials.	Completes short-term assignments, has most needed materials but does not plan long-term.	Completes short and long-term assignments in a timely manner; has needed materials and uses time wisely.	Plans schedule to include all priorities, completes all long and short term assignments, has needed materials and uses time wisely.

Strategies or Interventions *(Describe or list below)*

Formative Assessments *(Monitoring the Student's Response to Organizational Skills Interventions)*

Date _____

Test score _____   Checklist Indicator(s) _____

Observation(s)

Performance Assessment
Below Expectation..Exceeds Expectations

Demonstrates no skill in organizing materials, time, assignments or events.	Writes down assignments but procrastinates in doing them; often loses or does not have materials.	Completes short-term assignments, has most needed materials but does not plan long-term.	Completes short and long-term assignments in a timely manner; has needed materials and uses time wisely.	Plans schedule to include all priorities, completes all long and short term assignments, has needed materials and uses time wisely.

Date _____

Test score _____   Checklist Indicator(s) _____

Observation(s)

Performance Assessment
Below Expectation..Exceeds Expectations

Demonstrates no skill in organizing materials, time, assignments or events.	Writes down assignments but procrastinates in doing them; often loses or does not have materials.	Completes short-term assignments, has most needed materials but does not plan long-term.	Completes short and long-term assignments in a timely manner; has needed materials and uses time wisely.	Plans schedule to include all priorities, completes all long and short term assignments, has needed materials and uses time wisely.

Date _____

Test score _____   Checklist Indicator(s) _____

Observation(s)

Performance Assessment
Below Expectation..Exceeds Expectations

Demonstrates no skill in organizing materials, time, assignments or events.	Writes down assignments but procrastinates in doing them; often loses or does not have materials.	Completes short-term assignments, has most needed materials but does not plan long-term.	Completes short and long-term assignments in a timely manner; has needed materials and uses time wisely.	Plans schedule to include all priorities, completes all long and short term assignments, has needed materials and uses time wisely.

Summarize the Student's Response to Organizational Skills Interventions

Decision:

☐ Continue these interventions as needed and appropriate

☐ Modify the intervention:

☐ Select / implement a new intervention

☐ Move to the next tier (Tier _____)

☐ Refer for other special services:

Sequencing Skills

VIGNETTE: JOSÉ

SEQUENCING SKILLS INTERVENTIONS

SEQUENCING SKILLS RTI EXAMPLE

SEQUENCING SKILLS RTI FORM

JOSÉ

José is an active second grader. He is interested in everything but in a very random way. He starts something and then his attention is diverted to something else. Rarely does he do anything in a sequential order from beginning to end. This lack of sequencing skills is also evident in his schoolwork. He has difficulty identifying the beginning, middle, and ending of most stories. In math he is very accurate with simple computations but gets mixed up when problems require more than one step. In science and social studies he has a hard time knowing what event was first and/or the order of steps to take in using the scientific method. José needs help in developing sequencing skills in nearly every area of his life.

Using a quick Learning Styles checklist, José's teacher, Ms. Rodriguez, discovered that he was a Concrete Random learner (Gregorc, 1984). She brainstormed a number of possible approaches for teaching sequencing skills based on each of four learning modalities – Visual, Verbal, Kinesthetic, and Technological (page 107).

As an intervention for teaching sequencing skills during reading instruction, Ms. Rodriguez decided to use both time lines and storyboards to visually show how events are sequenced in stories. Over a six-week period she used these approaches with the whole class for each story they read. She found that José understood the storyboards more quickly than the timelines. After the third story, she assembled a small group of students including José and three other children who were also having trouble with sequencing skills. With this small group she began with storyboards and had the students in the group make time lines based on the storyboard information. This helped by showing them how these two strategies could be used together to learn to sequence any series of events whether they were fictional, historical, or current (such as a science observation).

In math problem solving where more than one step was required, Ms. Rodriguez decided to let José begin solving each problem (or group of problems) by generating a flowchart of the steps on the computer. As a motivational technique this worked well. José was excited about being allowed to use the computer. However, he did not have much success knowing what steps he should use when solving math problems. Therefore, his flowcharts were almost always inaccurate or useless.

At the end of six weeks Ms. Rodriguez decided to continue with the storyboard and time line strategies in reading, social studies, and science. She needed a new intervention for teaching steps in math problem solving.

Sequencing Skills Interventions

Depending on the student's learning preference, give him a choice of the following:

Visual

- Fill in a concept map showing ways you might solve a problem or reach a goal. Then number the steps in sequence.
- Develop a time line showing the sequence of 3-5 events.
- Create a storyboard showing the steps or parts of a story.

Verbal

- Plan a talk explaining four steps describing something you know how to do. Be specific by saying: First…, next…, then…, finally.
- Tell a story to another student, paraprofessional, or your teacher. Explain three or more events in the story, putting them in the correct order.

Kinesthetic

- Use flash cards, pictures, or any other manipulatives (for any subject or topic) and place them in the correct order.
- Act out in a skit or pantomime at least three parts of a story or concept.

Technological

- Create a flowchart showing four steps in doing something or four parts of a story or concept.
- Play a video game explaining the sequence of the steps as you play.

Coil RTI Progress Monitoring Form™
Sequencing Skills

Student's Name _____José_____

Targeted Skill, Knowledge, or Behavior
- Organizing facts, dates, numbers, events, etc. into the correct order
- Understanding that many things progress in an orderly, sequential way

Pre-assessment: *(Record all that apply)*

Date(s) of Pre-assessment _____

Test score(s) 30-50 %   **Checklist Indicator(s)** _____

Observation(s)

José's test scores reflect his random learning style. He never puts things in order or in a logical sequence. This is true for math computations, math problem solving, reading comprehension, and writing skills.

Performance Assessment

Below Expectation...Exceeds Expectations

Does not under-stand that facts items, dates, numbers, etc. can be arranged sequentially.	Has two items, ideas, dates, events or facts in the correct sequence.	Has less than half of the items, ideas, dates, events or facts in the correct sequence.	Has more than half of the items, ideas, dates, events or facts in the correct sequence.	Has all of the items, ideas, dates, events or facts in the correct sequence.

Strategies or Interventions *(Describe or list below)*

Strategies or Interventions	Person Responsible	Timeline
1. Use both storyboards and time lines to show the sequence of events in stories.	Classroom teacher (Whole class)	6 weeks
2. With a small group show how storyboards are related to time lines & can be used together.	Classroom teacher (Small group)	3 weeks
3. Use computer-generated flowcharts to write down steps in math problem solving.	Classroom teacher (Individual intervention)	3 weeks

Formative Assessments *(Monitoring the Student's Response to Sequencing Skills Interventions)*

Date After 3 weeks

Test score 40%
Math unit test

Checklist Indicator(s) _____

Observation(s)

José understood the sequences of the reading stories when they were presented in the storyboards. Beginning to generate his own. Unsuccessful using computer-generated flow-charts to see the steps in math problem solving.

Performance Assessment

Below Expectation...Exceeds Expectations

Doesn't under-stand that facts, items, dates, numbers, etc. can be sequential. **Math**	Has two items, ideas, dates, events or facts in the correct sequence.	Has less than half of the items, ideas, dates, events or facts in the correct sequence.	Has more than half of the items, ideas, dates, events or facts in the correct sequence. **(Reading)**	Has all of the items, ideas, dates, events or facts in the correct sequence.

Date End of 5 weeks

Test score 50-70%
Range of several test scores

Checklist Indicator(s) _____

Observation(s)

Small group work on storyboards and time lines for reading, science, and social studies is a successful intervention. Student has demonstrated a better understanding of sequencing in these areas in class work, homework, and tests.

Performance Assessment

Below Expectation...Exceeds Expectations

Does not under-stand that facts, items, dates, numbers, etc. can be arranged sequentially.	Has two items, ideas, dates, events or facts in the correct sequence.	Has less than half of the items, ideas, dates, events or facts in the correct sequence.	Has more than half of the items, ideas, dates, events or facts in the correct sequence. **Science, social studies & reading**	Has all of the items, ideas, dates, events or facts in the correct sequence.

Date End of 6 weeks

Test score _____

Checklist Indicator(s) _____

Observation(s)

Slight improvement in math sequencing. Continued improvement in other subject areas. Outline for writing assignment done in correct sequential order.

Performance Assessment

Below Expectation...Exceeds Expectations

Does not under-stand that facts, items, dates, numbers, etc. can be arranged sequentially.	Has two items, ideas, dates, events or facts in the correct sequence. **Occasionally in math**	Has less than half of the items, ideas, dates, events or facts in the correct sequence.	Has more than half of the items, ideas, dates, events or facts in the correct sequence. **Reading, writing, science & soc. st.**	Has all of the items, ideas, dates, events or facts in the correct sequence.

109

Summarize the Student's Response to Sequencing Skills Interventions

1. José responded well to the whole class intervention of using storyboards to show sequencing in fiction stories.

2. He benefitted from the small group instruction connecting storyboards to the development of time lines. Both of these interventions helped him understand sequencing more fully.

3. Average test scores in reading comprehension increased from 30%-50% to 50-70%.

4. The knowledge of sequencing skills learned in reading has transferred into other subject areas except math.

5. Generating flowcharts on the computer to learn steps in math problem solving was not a successful intervention. While the student was motivated by being able to work on the computer, he was unable to delineate the steps of the problem to put on the flowchart.

Decision:

X Continue the interventions as needed and appropriate

☐ Modify the intervention:

X Select / implement a new intervention

    Need to use another intervention to help this student understand the sequential steps in solving math problems.

☐ Move to the next tier (Tier _____)

☐ Refer for other special services:

Coil RTI Progress Monitoring Form™
Sequencing Skills

Student's Name _____

Targeted Skill, Knowledge, or Behavior
- **Organizing facts, dates, numbers, events, etc. into the correct order**
- **Understanding that many things progress in an orderly, sequential way**

Pre-assessment: *(Record all that apply)*

Date(s) of Pre-assessment _____

Test score(s) _____   **Checklist Indicator(s)** _____

Observation(s)

Performance Assessment
Below Expectation.. Exceeds Expectations

Does not understand that facts, items, dates, numbers, etc. can be arranged sequentially.	Has two items, ideas, dates, events or facts in the correct sequence.	Has less than half of the items, ideas, dates, events or facts in the correct sequence.	Has more than half of the items, ideas, dates, events or facts in the correct sequence.	Has all of the items, ideas, dates, events or facts in the correct sequence.

Strategies or Interventions *(Describe or list below)*

Formative Assessments *(Monitoring the Student's Response to Sequencing Skills Interventions)*

Date _____

Test score _____   Checklist Indicator(s) _____

Observation(s)

Performance Assessment
Below Expectation..Exceeds Expectations

Does not under-stand that facts, items, dates, numbers, etc. can be arranged sequentially.	Has two items, ideas, dates, events or facts in the correct sequence.	Has less than half of the items, ideas, dates, events or facts in the correct sequence.	Has more than half of the items, ideas, dates, events or facts in the correct sequence.	Has all of the items, ideas, dates, events or facts in the correct sequence.

Date _____

Test score _____   Checklist Indicator(s) _____

Observation(s)

Performance Assessment
Below Expectation..Exceeds Expectations

Does not under-stand that facts, items, dates, numbers, etc. can be arranged sequentially.	Has two items, ideas, dates, events or facts in the correct sequence.	Has less than half of the items, ideas, dates, events or facts in the correct sequence.	Has more than half of the items, ideas, dates, events or facts in the correct sequence.	Has all of the items, ideas, dates, events or facts in the correct sequence.

Date _____

Test score _____   Checklist Indicator(s) _____

Observation(s)

Performance Assessment
Below Expectation..Exceeds Expectations

Does not under-stand that facts, items, dates, numbers, etc. can be arranged sequentially.	Has two items, ideas, dates, events or facts in the correct sequence.	Has less than half of the items, ideas, dates, events or facts in the correct sequence.	Has more than half of the items, ideas, dates, events or facts in the correct sequence.	Has all of the items, ideas, dates, events or facts in the correct sequence.

Summarize the Student's Response to Sequencing Skills Interventions

Decision:

☐ Continue the interventions as needed and appropriate

☐ Modify the intervention:

☐ Select / implement a new intervention

☐ Move to the next tier (Tier _____)

☐ Refer for other special services:

Test-Taking Skills

VIGNETTE: JERMAINE

JERMAINE'S ACHIEVEMENT CHARACTERISTICS CHECKLIST

TEST-TAKING SKILLS (MEMORIZATION TECHNIQUES) RTI EXAMPLE

TEST-TAKING SKILLS (MEMORIZATION TECHNIQUES) RTI FORM

JERMAINE

Jermaine is a middle school student who is failing unit tests and quizzes in most subjects. He also does poorly on the high stakes standardized tests given by the state each year. Furthermore, his school uses benchmark assessments that have the same format as the yearly test, and he doesn't perform well on these either. Jermaine's contributions to class discussion demonstrate his general knowledge on a wide range of topics, but he does not memorize the knowledge base and details that are often asked on tests. There are a number of test-taking skills that Jermaine needs to work on. His teacher believes he could do better on tests if he masters these skills.

"Students who are test-wise can outperform students of equal ability who lack test-wiseness." – **Scruggs & Mastropieri (1992)**

Years of research have shown that positive test score gains can be achieved by teaching students test-taking skills and techniques. Jermaine needs to learn specific test-taking strategies in order to do better on the many tests he is required to take. Test-taking strategies work best when they are specific to the test or tests the student will be taking. In general, the current testing environment involves two types of tests: **multiple choice** from a menu of possible correct answers and **open-ended responses** where the child must construct his or her own answers.

In this book you will find five *Coil RTI Progress Monitoring Forms™* designed specifically for test-taking skills. These include:

- Following Directions (page 161)
- Memorization Techniques (page 120)
- Multiple Choice Techniques (page 164)
- Reading the Questions (page 167)
- Time Management Techniques (page 170)

These forms work a bit differently from the other Progress Monitoring Forms found in this book. In the other cases, growth is seen as a definite sequential progression within a skill set. Test-taking skills are broader and more numerous. They are also somewhat based on individual preference. For example, one student may memorize new information by making up a song that includes unfamiliar vocabulary while another might put the unfamiliar words into categories and memorize them in that way. Because of this, the Performance Assessments for Test-Taking Skills begin with a box describing below average expectations. The other boxes indicate different test-taking techniques. Students who are good test takers generally master more than one of the techniques indicated. Progress is monitored by circling the appropriate box for each technique used.

Jermaine's teacher decided to use interventions that focused on the test-taking skill of Memorization Techniques. Jermaine used two of these, and his test scores improved somewhat. He needs to use other test-taking techniques to continue this improvement.

RTI Achievement Characteristics Checklist

Directions: *Rate the targeted student using the following indicators.*
You may leave some items blank.

W =	Weak in this area
I =	Improving in this area
S =	Strong in this area

Name of student: ____Jermaine_____

— 1.   Exhibits good organizational and time management skills.

— 2.   Turns assignments in on time.

S 3.   Is punctual and has good attendance.

— 4.   Is persistent when working on tasks that don't come easily.

I 5.   Is willing to redo work when it is not correct the first time.

— 6.   Shows pride in the quality of his/her schoolwork.

— 7.   Is willing to obtain help in remediation of an academic weakness.

W 8.   Works to improve when grades or test scores are low.

— 9.   Finds at least one topic/subject at school that he/she feels is interesting and worthwhile.

W 10. Knows strategies for memorizing unfamiliar information.

— 11. Has a good attention span and can concentrate on learning.

— 12. Shows creativity at home or at school.

— 13. Can think logically to solve academic problems.

— 14. Sets short- and long-term goals.

— 15. Sees the relationship between achievement in school and future success.

Specific behaviors can be identified and targeted by using this checklist. You can also identify patterns of positive or negative behaviors.

Coil RTI Progress Monitoring Form™
Test-Taking Skills: Memorization Techniques

Student's Name Jermaine

Targeted Skill, Knowledge, or Behavior
- Ability to remember important facts, ideas and information
- Ability to record important information for review at a later time

Pre-assessment: (Record all that apply)

Date(s) of Pre-assessment _____

Test score(s) <u>20%, 25%</u> Checklist Indicator(s) <u>RTI Achievement Characteristics</u>
        On unit tests   Weaknesses in #8 & #10

Observation(s)

> Student misses knowledge-based questions. Does not know how to memorize information he does not already know.

Performance Assessment

(Below Expectation) The more techniques circled in boxes 2-5 below, the more this skill is mastered.

Box # 1	Box # 2	Box # 3	Box # 4	Box # 5
Demonstrates no ability to organize or relate to unfamiliar information in order to memorize it.	Can relate unfamiliar information to things he already knows.	Is able to put unfamiliar information into a song, poem or other mnemonic device in order to learn it.	Organizes unfamiliar information into categories in order to learn it.	Makes flash cards, notes or index cards and reviews them often in order to learn unfamiliar information.

Strategies or Interventions (Describe or list below)

Intervention or Strategy	Person Responsible	Timeline
1. Have student develop flash cards and eview information with a partner.	Classroom teacher	5 weeks
2. Whole class instruction on learning new information using mnemonic devices.	Classroom teacher	2 weeks

Formative Assessments *(Monitoring the Student's Response to Memorization Techniques Interventions)*

Date after 2 weeks

Test score _____   Checklist Indicator(s) _____

Observation(s)

    Student is willing and able to make flash cards if he is given a list of those to write. He has not practiced with a partner but reviews on his own.

Performance Assessment

[Below Expectation]   The more techniques circled in boxes 2-5 below, the more this skill is mastered.

Box # 1	Box # 2	Box # 3	Box # 4	Box # 5
Demonstrates no ability to organize or relate to unfamiliar information in order to memorize it.	Can relate unfamiliar information to things he already knows.	Is able to put unfamiliar information into a song, poem or other mnemonic device in order to learn it.	Organizes unfamiliar information into categories in order to learn it.	Makes flash cards, notes or index cards and reviews them often in order to learn unfamiliar information.

Date after 4 weeks

Test score 40%-50%   Checklist Indicator(s) RTI Achievement Characteristics
Range of scores on tests   Improving in #8 & #10

Observation(s)

    He reviews flashcards sporadically. Worked with a partner twice in four weeks. Using flash cards needs to be a regular habit. Test scores should be higher.

Performance Assessment

[Below Expectation]   The more techniques circled in boxes 2-5 below, the more this skill is mastered.

Box #1	Box # 2	Box # 3	Box # 4	Box # 5
Demonstrates no ability to organize or relate to unfamiliar information in order to memorize it.	Can relate unfamiliar information to things he already knows.	Is able to put unfamiliar information into a song, poem or other mnemonic device in order to learn it.	Organizes unfamiliar information into categories in order to learn it.	Makes flash cards, notes or index cards and **reviews them often (NO)** in order to learn unfamiliar information.

Date after 5 weeks

Test score 55%   Checklist Indicator(s) RTI Achievement Characteristics
    Science unit test   Improving in #8 & #10

Observation(s)

    Test scores are slowly improving. Learned some of the information contained in class song on the Periodic Table as evidenced by somewhat higher test score.

Performance Assessment

[Below Expectation]   The more techniques circled in boxes 2-5 below, the more this skill is mastered.

Box # 1	Box # 2	Box # 3	Box # 4	Box # 5
Demonstrates no ability to organize or relate to unfamiliar information in order to memorize it.	Can relate unfamiliar information to things he already knows.	Is able to put unfamiliar information into a song, poem or other mnemonic device in order to learn it.	Organizes unfamiliar information into categories in order to learn it.	Makes flash cards, notes or index cards and reviews them often in order to learn unfamiliar information.

Summarize the Student's Response to Memorization Techniques Intervention(s)

1. Learned some information by using the flash cards and mnemonic devices (class song).

2. Test scores are higher (55% on science test) but not near mastery.

3. Jermaine's RTI Achievement Characteristics Checklist shows improvement in working when test scores are low and in knowing strategies for learning unfamiliar information.

4. Student needs to use these strategies regularly.

Decision:

X Continue the interventions as needed and appropriate
    Continue to add more memorization techniques.

X Modify the intervention:
    Daily flash card work for 15 minutes with a student partner or paraprofessional. This needs to be every day.

☐ Select / implement a new intervention
    Use and monitor another test-taking skill:
        Following directions
        Multiple Choice Techniques
        Reading the Questions,
        Time Management Techniques
☐ Move to the next tier (Tier _____)

☐ Refer for other special services:

Coil RTI Progress Monitoring Form™
Test-Taking Skills: Memorization Techniques

Student's Name _____

Targeted Skill, Knowledge, or Behavior
- **Ability to remember important facts, ideas and information**
- **Ability to record important information for review at a later time**

Pre-assessment: *(Record all that apply)*

Date(s) of Pre-assessment _____

Test score(s) _____   Checklist Indicator(s) _____

Observation(s) _____

Performance Assessment

(Below Expectation) The more techniques circled in boxes 2-5 below, the more this skill is mastered.

Box # 1	Box # 2	Box # 3	Box # 4	Box # 5
Demonstrates no ability to organize or relate to unfamiliar information in order to memorize it.	Can relate unfamiliar information to things he already knows.	Is able to put unfamiliar information into a song, poem or other mnemonic device in order to learn it.	Organizes unfamiliar information into categories in order to learn it.	Makes flash cards, notes or index cards and reviews them often in order to learn unfamiliar information.

Strategies or Interventions *(Describe or list below)*

Intervention or Strategy   **Person Responsible**   **Timeline**

120

Formative Assessments *(Monitoring the Student's Response to Memorization Techniques Interventions)*

Date _____

Test score _____   Checklist Indicator(s) _____

Observation(s)

Performance Assessment
[Below Expectation]   The more techniques circled in boxes 2-5 below, the more this skill is mastered.

Box # 1	Box # 2	Box # 3	Box # 4	Box # 5
Demonstrates no ability to organize or relate to unfamiliar information in order to memorize it.	Can relate unfamiliar information to things he already knows.	Is able to put unfamiliar information into a song, poem or other mnemonic device in order to learn it.	Organizes unfamiliar information into categories in order to learn it.	Makes flash cards, notes or index cards and reviews them often in order to learn unfamiliar information.

Date _____

Test score _____   Checklist Indicator(s) _____

Observation(s)

Performance Assessment
[Below Expectation]   The more techniques circled in boxes 2-5 below, the more this skill is mastered.

Box # 1	Box # 2	Box # 3	Box # 4	Box # 5
Demonstrates no ability to organize or relate to unfamiliar information in order to memorize it.	Can relate unfamiliar information to things he already knows.	Is able to put unfamiliar information into a song, poem or other mnemonic device in order to learn it.	Organizes unfamiliar information into categories in order to learn it.	Makes flash cards, notes or index cards and reviews them often in order to learn unfamiliar information.

Date _____

Test score _____   Checklist Indicator(s) _____

Observation(s)

Performance Assessment
[Below Expectation]   The more techniques circled in boxes 2-5 below, the more this skill is mastered.

Box # 1	Box # 2	Box # 3	Box # 4	Box # 5
Demonstrates no ability to organize or relate to unfamiliar information in order to memorize it.	Can relate unfamiliar information to things he already knows.	Is able to put unfamiliar information into a song, poem or other mnemonic device in order to learn it.	Organizes unfamiliar information into categories in order to learn it.	Makes flash cards, notes or index cards and reviews them often in order to learn unfamiliar information.

Summarize the Student's Response to Memorization Techniques Intervention(s)

Decision:

☐ Continue the interventions as needed and appropriate

☐ Modify the intervention:

☐ Select / implement a new intervention

☐ Move to the next tier (Tier _____)

☐ Refer for other special services:

Tiered Lessons and Units

VIGNETTE: NOAH AND LOGAN

COMPOUND WORDS TIERED LESSON PLAN

TIERED LESSON LEVEL 1 RTI EXAMPLE

TIERED LESSON LEVEL 1 RTI FORM

TIERED LESSON LEVEL 3 RTI EXAMPLE

TIERED LESSON LEVEL 3 RTI FORM

NOAH AND LOGAN

Noah and Logan are both in the same first grade class. Noah struggles in school, particularly with reading and language. He reads at a kindergarten level even though he is more than half way through first grade. On the other hand, Logan is an excellent reader and writer. He reads independently on a third grade level and has even tried to read some books at a fourth grade reading level. Their teacher needs to teach the same language arts standards to both students. She doesn't want Noah to be lost and confused, but she also doesn't want Logan to be bored or unchallenged.

One of the most effective research-based differentiation strategies to use in a classroom where students are functioning at different levels yet need to learn the same standards is Tiered Lessons and Units. This is a particularly strong RTI intervention because by its very nature, it allows lessons in the general education classroom to be taught at different levels of readiness, knowledge, or ability. Each level targets specific students in the classroom.

The levels in tiered lessons and units should not be confused with RTI tiers. Tiered lessons generally have three levels. In each of these levels, students work on the grade-level standards. Level 1 scaffolds the standards and makes them easier to understand and accomplish. Level 2 is generally the grade-level activity or activities you would normally do if you were not tiering the lesson or unit. Level 3 extends the thinking and challenges your top students.

Tiered lessons and units can take any length of time to teach. Regardless of the time involved, the format remains the same:

- List of objectives or standards to be accomplished by all students
- Whole class activities
- Leveled activities
- Whole class culminating activities

All activities should be respectful learning activities. As much as possible, the leveled activities should be similar to each other. One important consideration is not to make Level 3 activities simply more of the same work. Instead, they should be more challenging with additional rigor and higher-level thinking.

On the next two pages is a Tiered Lesson on Compound Words Noah and Logan's teacher used. Noah did Level 1 activities while Logan did Level 3. Both accomplished the stated standards and objectives. Both learned new things and were challenged. Note the progress of each student on their Tiered Lesson Progress Monitoring Forms.

Tiered Lesson Plan: Compound Words

Objectives or Standards

1. Students will recognize the structure of compound words.
2. Students will understand how and when compound words are used.
3. Students will create and use compound words.

Whole Class Activities

1. Demonstrate how compound words are created by using puzzle pieces with simple words to make compound words.

2. Listen to and sing the "Grammar Rock" song on compound words.

Assessment

❑All look and listen to teacher's demonstration.

❑All students singing and participating.

Level 3 Activities

1. Have these students make their own compound words from the puzzle pieces and write them on a sheet of paper.

2. Write 10 sentences using these compound words.

Assessment

❑All words created are compound words.

❑Correct spelling of words.
❑All words used.
❑Has 10 sentences.

Level 2 Activities

1. Generate a list of 10 new compound words. Highlight each part of the compound word with a different color.

2. Write two paragraphs using all 10 words.

Assessment

❑Has 10 compound words.
❑Parts are indicated correctly.

❑Paragraphs are in correct form with main idea.
❑All 10 words used.

from Activities & Assessments for the Differentiated Classroom. Carolyn Coil.
Pieces of Learning. www.piecesoflearning.com

Level 3 Activities

1. Make a dictionary with 10 original compound words. Define and illustrate each.

2. Write a short story using these 10 words.

Assessment

☞ ❑Has 10 original words and definitions.
❑Words are illustrated.
❑In alphabetical order.

☞ ❑Story uses all 10 words.
❑Has a plot with a beginning, middle and end.

Whole Class Culminating Activities

1. Share products from Levels 1, 2 and 3.

2. "Walking Words" activity where each student holds a word and finds a partner to make a compound word.

Assessment

❑Group participation

from Activities & Assessments for the Differentiated Classroom. Carolyn Coil.
Pieces of Learning. www.piecesoflearning.com

Coil RTI Progress Monitoring Form™
Tiered Lessons – Level 1

Student's Name _____ Noah _____

Targeted Skill, Knowledge, or Behavior
- Any academic skill or standard that must be mastered: Compound Words

---

Pre-assessment: *(Record all that apply)*

Date(s) of Pre-assessment _____

Test score(s) ____20%____ Checklist Indicator(s) _____
Identification of compound words

Observation(s)

In informal discussions, this student demonstrates little knowledge of compound words and how they are formed.

Performance Assessment
Below Expectation...Exceeds Expectations

Student is lost during whole class instruction and doesn't know how to begin, work on, or complete the assignment.	Student begins the work and shows some understanding of the topic when taught in a smaller group using a Tiered Lesson Plan format.	Student understands most of the topic and can do some of the work when taught in a smaller group using a Tiered Lesson Plan format.	Student understands most of the topic and completes the work when taught in a smaller group using a Tiered Lesson Plan format.	Student understands and masters the topic or skill and accurately completes the work when taught in a smaller group using a Tiered Lesson Plan format.

Strategies or Interventions: *(Describe or list below)*

Use the Compound Words Tiered Lesson Plan - Level 1

— Whole group activities

— List of compound words using puzzle pieces

— Sentences with compound words

— Walking words

Formative Assessments *(Monitoring the Student's Response to Tiered Lessons)*

Date _____

Test score _____ Checklist Indicator(s) _____

Observation(s)

Student participated with interest during the puzzle pieces activity.

Performance Assessment

Below Expectation...Exceeds Expectations

Student is lost during whole class instruction and doesn't know how to begin, work on, or complete the assignment.	Student begins the work and shows some understanding of the topic when taught in a smaller group using a Tiered Lesson Plan format.	Student understands most of the topic and can do some of the work when taught in a smaller group using a Tiered Lesson Plan format.	Student understands most of the topic and completes the work when taught in a smaller group using a Tiered Lesson Plan format.	Student understands and masters the topic or skill and accurately completes the work when taught in a smaller group using a Tiered Lesson Plan format.

Date _____

Test score _____ Checklist Indicator(s) __Completed list of 10 words_____

Observation(s)

Understands the structure of compound words

Performance Assessment   word structure

Below Expectation...Exceeds Expectations

Student is lost during whole class instruction and doesn't know how to begin, work on, or complete the assignment.	Student begins the work and shows some understanding of the topic when taught in a smaller group using a Tiered Lesson Plan format.	Student understands most of the topic and can do some of the work when taught in a smaller group using a Tiered Lesson Plan format.	Student understands most of the topic and completes the work when taught in a smaller group using a Tiered Lesson Plan format.	Student understands and masters the topic or skill and accurately completes the work when taught in a smaller group using a Tiered Lesson Plan format.

Date _____

Test score ___70%___ Checklist Indicator(s) __Found partner in walking words__

Identification of compound words

Observation(s)

Worked on sentences using the list of 10 words.

Struggles with sentence structure.

Performance Assessment sentence structure

Below Expectation...Exceeds Expectations

Student is lost during whole class instruction and doesn't know how to begin, work on, or complete the assignment.	Student begins the work and shows some understanding of the topic when taught in a smaller group using a Tiered Lesson Plan format.	Student understands most of the topic and can do some of the work when taught in a smaller group using a Tiered Lesson Plan format.	Student understands most of the topic and completes the work when taught in a smaller group using a Tiered Lesson Plan format.	Student understands and masters the topic or skill and accurately completes the work when taught in a smaller group using a Tiered Lesson Plan format.

128

Summarize the Student's Response to Tiered Lessons and Units Interventions

1. Test score increased from 20% to 70% on identification of compound words.

2. Student was able to complete activities focusing on the structure of compound words.

3. Needs more instruction on sentence structure.

Decision:

Continue tiered lessons as needed and appropriate

x   Modify the intervention:

Use tiered lessons for sentence structure.

Select / implement a new intervention

Move to the next tier (Tier _____)

Refer for other special services:

Coil RTI Progress Monitoring Form™
Tiered Lessons – Level 1

Student's Name _____

Targeted Skill, Knowledge, or Behavior
- **Any academic skill or standard that must be mastered:** _____

Pre-assessment: *(Record all that apply)*

Date(s) of Pre-assessment _____

Test score(s) _____ Checklist Indicator(s) _____

Observation(s) _____

Performance Assessment

Below Expectation ....Exceeds Expectations

Student is lost during whole class instruction and doesn't know how to begin, work on, or complete the assignment.	Student begins the work and shows some understanding of the topic when taught in a smaller group using a Tiered Lesson Plan format.	Student understands most of the topic and can do some of the work when taught in a smaller group using a Tiered Lesson Plan format.	Student understands most of the topic and completes the work when taught in a smaller group using a Tiered Lesson Plan format.	Student understands and masters the topic or skill and accurately completes the work when taught in a smaller group using a Tiered Lesson Plan format.

Strategies or Interventions: *(Describe or list below)*

Formative Assessments *(Monitoring the Student's Response to Tiered Lessons)*

Date _____

Test score _____ Checklist Indicator(s) _____

Observation(s)

Performance Assessment
Below Expectation...Exceeds Expectations

Student is lost during whole class instruction and doesn't know how to begin, work on, or complete the assignment.	Student begins the work and shows some understanding of the topic when taught in a smaller group using a Tiered Lesson Plan format.	Student understands most of the topic and can do some of the work when taught in a smaller group using a Tiered Lesson Plan format.	Student understands most of the topic and completes the work when taught in a smaller group using a Tiered Lesson Plan format.	Student understands and masters the topic or skill and accurately completes the work when taught in a smaller group using a Tiered Lesson Plan format.

Date _____

Test score _____ Checklist Indicator(s) _____

Observation(s)

Performance Assessment
Below Expectations...Exceeds Expectations

Student is lost during whole class instruction and doesn't know how to begin, work on, or complete the assignment.	Student begins the work and shows some understanding of the topic when taught in a smaller group using a Tiered Lesson Plan format.	Student understands most of the topic and can do some of the work when taught in a smaller group using a Tiered Lesson Plan format.	Student understands most of the topic and completes the work when taught in a smaller group using a Tiered Lesson Plan format.	Student understands and masters the topic or skill and accurately completes the work when taught in a smaller group using a Tiered Lesson Plan format.

Date _____

Test score _____ Checklist Indicator(s) _____

Observation(s)

Performance Assessment
Below Expectation...Exceeds Expectations

Student is lost during whole class instruction and doesn't know how to begin, work on, or complete the assignment.	Student begins the work and shows some understanding of the topic when taught in a smaller group using a Tiered Lesson Plan format.	Student understands most of the topic and can do some of the work when taught in a smaller group using a Tiered Lesson Plan format.	Student understands most of the topic and completes the work when taught in a smaller group using a Tiered Lesson Plan format.	Student understands and masters the topic or skill and accurately completes the work when taught in a smaller group using a Tiered Lesson Plan format.

Summarize the Student's Response to Tiered Lessons and Units Interventions

Decision:

☐ Continue tiered lessons as needed and appropriate

☐ Modify the intervention:

☐ Select / implement a new intervention

☐ Move to the next tier (Tier _____)

☐ Refer for other special services:

Coil RTI Progress Monitoring Form™
Tiered Lessons – Level 3

Student's Name _____ Logan _____

Targeted Skill, Knowledge, or Behavior
- Any academic skill or standard that must be mastered: Compound Words

Pre-assessment: *(Record all that apply)*

Date(s) of Pre-assessment _____

Test score(s) 90%   Checklist Indicator(s) _____
Identification of compound words

Observation(s)

Student understands structure of compound words and knows how to use them. He is an excellent reader and writer.

Performance Assessment

Below Expectation..Exceeds Expectations

Student understands most of the topic or skill as indicated by pretest, checklist or observation.	Student understands almost all of the topic or skill as indicated by pretest, checklist or observation.	Student has mastered the topic or skill as indicated by pretest, checklist or observation. Needs to be challenged beyond this skill.	Student extends his/her knowledge or skill by working in Level 3 of the Tiered Lesson Plan format.	Student demonstrates higher level thinking, makes connections with other areas of learning, and uses advanced resources in his/her work.

Strategies or Interventions: *(Describe or list below)*

Use the Compound Words Tiered Lesson Plan – Level 3
- Whole group activities : Puzzle Pieces
- Dictionary of compound words
- Short story using imaginary compound words
- Walking words activity

Formative Assessments *(Monitoring the Student's Response to Tiered Lessons)*

Date _____

Test score _____ Checklist Indicator(s) _____

Observation(s)

Student participated in and enjoyed the whole group Puzzle Piece activity

Performance Assessment

Below Expectation..Exceeds Expectations

Student understands most of the topic or skill as indicated by pretest, checklist or observation.	Student understands almost all of the topic or skill as indicated by pretest, checklist or observation.	Student has mastered the topic or skill as indicated by pretest, checklist or observation. Needs to be challenged beyond this skill.	Student extends his/her knowledge or skill by working in Level 3 of the Tiered Lesson Plan format.	Student demonstrates higher level thinking, makes connections with other areas of learning, and uses advanced resources in his/her work.

Date _____

Test score _____ Checklist Indicator(s) _____

Observation(s)

Was challenged when developing the dictionary.
Difficulty in creative thinking.

Performance Assessment

Below Expectation..Exceeds Expectations

Student understands most of the topic or skill as indicated by pretest, checklist or observation.	Student understands almost all of the topic or skill as indicated by pretest, checklist or observation.	Student has mastered the topic or skill as indicated by pretest, checklist or observation. Needs to be challenged beyond this skill.	Student extends his/her knowledge or skill by working in Level 3 of the Tiered Lesson Plan format.	Student demonstrates higher level thinking, makes connections with other areas of learning, and uses advanced resources in his/her work.

Date _____

Test score _100%_____ Checklist Indicator(s) _____

Identification of compound words

Observation(s)

Challenged throughout tiered unit.
Higher-level thinking demonstrated in short story.

Performance Assessment

Below Expectation..Exceeds Expectations

Student understands most of the topic or skill as indicated by pretest, checklist or observation.	Student understands almost all of the topic or skill as indicated by pretest, checklist or observation.	Student has mastered the topic or skill as indicated by pretest, checklist or observation. Needs to be challenged beyond this skill.	Student extends his/her knowledge or skill by working in Level 3 of the Tiered Lesson Plan format.	Student demonstrates higher level thinking, makes connections with other areas of learning, and uses advanced resources in his/her work.

Summarize the Student's Response to Tiered Lessons and Units

1. Demonstrated mastery of structure of compound words. (90% - 100%)

2. Level 3 activities challenged this student.

3. Extended learning in creativity, word usage, and storytelling.

Decision:

X Successfully mastered the targeted skill, knowledge or behavior.

X Continue tiered lessons as needed and appropriate

    Continue to challenge this student with Level 3 tiered activities.

☐ Modify the intervention:

☐ Select / implement a new intervention

☐ Move to the next tier (Tier _____)

☐ Refer for other special services:

Coil RTI Progress Monitoring Form™
Tiered Lessons – Level 3

Student's Name _____

Targeted Skill, Knowledge, or Behavior
- **Any academic skill or standard that must be mastered:** _____

Pre-assessment: *(Record all that apply)*

Date(s) of Pre-assessment _____

Test score(s) _____ Checklist Indicator(s) _____

Observation(s)

Performance Assessment

Below Expectation..Exceeds Expectations

Student understands most of the topic or skill as indicated by pretest, checklist or observation.	Student understands almost all of the topic or skill as indicated by pretest, checklist or observation.	Student has mastered the topic or skill as indicated by pretest, checklist or observation. Needs to be challenged beyond this skill.	Student extends his/her knowledge or skill by working in Level 3 of the Tiered Lesson Plan format.	Student demonstrates higher level thinking, makes connections with other areas of learning, and uses advanced resources in his/her work.

Strategies or Interventions: *(Describe or list below)*

Formative Assessments *(Monitoring the Student's Response to Tiered Lessons)*

Date _____

Test score _____ Checklist Indicator(s) _____

Observation(s)

Performance Assessment

Below Expectation...Exceeds Expectations

Student under-stands most of the topic or skill as indicated by pretest, checklist or observation.	Student understands almost all of the topic or skill as indicated by pretest, checklist or observation.	Student has mastered the topic or skill as indicated by pretest, checklist or observation. Needs to be challenged beyond this skill.	Student extends his/her knowledge or skill by working in Level 3 of the Tiered Lesson Plan format.	Student demonstrates higher level thinking, makes connections with other areas of learning, and uses advanced resources in his/her work.

Date _____

Test score _____ Checklist Indicator(s) _____

Observation(s)

Performance Assessment

Below Expectation..Exceeds Expectations

Student under-stands most of the topic or skill as indicated by pret-est, checklist or observation.	Student understands almost all of the top-ic or skill as indi-cated by pretest, checklist or observa-tion.	Student has mastered the topic or skill as indicated by pretest, checklist or observa-tion. Needs to be challenged beyond this skill.	Student extends his/her knowledge or skill by working in Level 3 of the Tiered Lesson Plan format.	Student demonstrates higher level thinking, makes connections with other areas of learning, and uses advanced resources in his/her work.

Date _____

Test score _____ Checklist Indicator(s) _____

Observation(s)

Performance Assessment

Below Expectation...Exceeds Expectations

Student under-stands most of the topic or skill as indicated by pret-est, checklist or observation.	Student understands almost all of the top-ic or skill as indi-cated by pretest, checklist or observa-tion.	Student has mas-tered the topic or skill as indicated by pret-est, checklist or ob-servation. Needs to be challenged beyond this skill.	Student extends his/her knowledge or skill by working in Level 3 of the Tiered Lesson Plan format.	Student demonstrates higher level thinking, makes connections with other areas of learning, and uses advanced resources in his/her work.

Summarize the Student's Response to Tiered Lessons and Units

Decision:

☐ Continue tiered lessons as needed and appropriate

☐ Modify the intervention:

☐ Select / implement a new intervention

☐ Move to the next tier (Tier _____)

☐ Refer for other special services:

Introduction to other Coil RTI Progress Monitoring Forms™

Throughout this book you have read vignettes of students and learned how their teachers monitored their progress using various *Coil RTI Progress Monitoring Forms™*. After each example there was a blank form of the same type for you to use with your own students. These forms can be used exactly as they are written, or you can use the CD to modify them in WORD and print out your own version. There are thirteen different *Coil RTI Progress Monitoring Forms™*.

The next section of this book has ten additional *Coil RTI Progress Monitoring Forms™*. They cover a large variety of needs, concerns, and interventions. Use them in the same way the others have been used throughout this book. Also incorporated into this section is a blank *Coil RTI Progress Monitoring Form™* for you to write your own.

The three-page *Coil RTI Progress Monitoring Forms™* included in this section of the book are:

- Blank RTI Form
- Comprehension skills: Listening and Speaking
- Comprehension skills: Reading and Writing
- Math Problem Solving
- Phonemic Awareness
- Self Confidence
- Spelling/Vocabulary Patterns
- Test-Taking Skills: Following Directions
- Test-Taking Skills: Multiple Choice techniques
- Test-Taking Skills: Reading the Questions
- Test-Taking Skills: Time Management

Coil RTI Progress Monitoring Form™
Need/Concern or Intervention _____

Student's Name _____

Targeted Skill, Knowledge, or Behavior

Pre-assessment: *(Record all that apply)*

Date(s) of Pre-assessment _____

Test score(s) _____   Checklist Indicator(s) _____

Observation(s) _____

Performance Assessment

Below Expectation...Exceeds Expectations

Strategies or Interventions *(Describe or list below)*

Formative Assessments *(Monitoring the Student's Response to the Intervention)*

Date _____

Test score _____   Checklist Indicator(s) _____

Observation(s)

Performance Assessment
Below Expectation...Exceeds Expectations

Date _____

Test score _____   Checklist Indicator(s) _____

Observation(s)

Performance Assessment
Below Expectation...Exceeds Expectations

Date _____

Test score _____   Checklist Indicator(s) _____

Observation(s)

Performance Assessment
Below Expectation...Exceeds Expectations

Summarize the Student's Response to the Intervention(s)

Decision:

☐ Continue these interventions as needed and appropriate

☐ Modify the intervention:

☐ Select / implement a new intervention

☐ Move to the next tier (Tier _____)

☐ Refer for other special services:

Coil RTI Progress Monitoring Form™
Comprehension: Listening & Speaking

Student's Name _____

Targeted Skill, Knowledge, or Behavior
- **Listens to story or other information and can explain it aloud**
- **Shows understanding through drawing**

Pre-assessment: *(Record all that apply)*

Date(s) of Pre-assessment _____

Test score(s) _____Checklist Indicator(s) _____

Observation(s) _____

Performance Assessment

Below Expectation..Exceeds Expectations

Does not pay attention to the story or information. Unable to show comprehension.	Pays attention to the story or information (eye contact, nods, etc.) but cannot explain it verbally or draw pictures of it.	Pays attention to the story or information and can show understanding through drawings.	Pays attention to the story or information and can accurately tell about it thereby showing understanding.	Pays attention to the story or information, can tell about it accurately and asks higher level thinking questions to learn more.

Strategies or Interventions *(Describe or list below)*

Formative Assessments *(Monitoring the Student's Response to Listening/Speaking Interventions)*

Date _____

Test score _____   Checklist Indicator(s) _____

Observation(s)

Performance Assessment
Below Expectation..Exceeds Expectations

Does not pay attention to the story or information. Unable to show comprehension.	Pays attention to the story or information (eye contact, nods, etc.) but cannot explain it verbally or draw pictures of it.	Pays attention to the story or information and can show understanding through drawings.	Pays attention to the story or information and can accurately tell about it thereby showing understanding.	Pays attention to the story or information, can tell about it accurately and asks higher level thinking questions to learn more.

Date _____

Test score _____   Checklist Indicator(s) _____

Observation(s)

Performance Assessment
Below Expectation..Exceeds Expectations

Does not pay attention to the story or information. Unable to show comprehension.	Pays attention to the story or information (eye contact, nods, etc.) but cannot explain it verbally or draw pictures of it.	Pays attention to the story or information and can show understanding through drawings.	Pays attention to the story or information and can accurately tell about it thereby showing understanding.	Pays attention to the story or information, can tell about it accurately and asks higher level thinking questions to learn more.

Date _____

Test score _____   Checklist Indicator(s) _____

Observation(s)

Performance Assessment
Below Expectation..Exceeds Expectations

Does not pay attention to the story or information. Unable to show comprehension.	Pays attention to the story or information (eye contact, nods, etc.) but cannot explain it verbally or draw pictures of it.	Pays attention to the story or information and can show understanding through drawings.	Pays attention to the story or information and can accurately tell about it thereby showing understanding.	Pays attention to the story or information, can tell about it accurately and asks higher level thinking questions to learn more.

Summarize the Student's Response to Listening & Speaking Interventions

Decision:

☐ Continue these interventions as needed and appropriate

☐ Modify the intervention:

☐ Select / implement a new intervention

☐ Move to the next tier (Tier _____)

☐ Refer for other special services:

Coil RTI Progress Monitoring Form™
Comprehension: Reading & Writing

Student's Name _____

Targeted Skill, Knowledge, or Behavior
- **Reads the story or other information and can explain it in written form**
- **Shows understanding and gives feedback through writing**

Pre-assessment: *(Record all that apply)*

Date(s) of Pre-assessment _____

Test score(s) _____   Checklist Indicator(s) _____

Observation(s)

Performance Assessment
Below Expectation ....Exceeds Expectations

Unable to decode the words. Cannot explain what the reading was about in any written form.	Can decode the words and can orally explain what the reading was about but cannot write an explanation.	Can read aloud or silently and can write a brief sentence that shows some understanding of what was read.	Can read aloud or silently and can write two or more sentences that show some understanding of what was read.	Can read aloud or silently and can write a detailed explanation that shows a good understanding of what was read.

Strategies or Interventions *(Describe or list below)*

Formative Assessments _(Monitoring the Student's Response to Reading/ Writing Interventions)_

Date _____

Test score _____   Checklist Indicator(s) _____

Observation(s)

Performance Assessment
Below Expectation..Exceeds Expectations

Unable to decode the words. Cannot explain what the reading was about in any written form.	Can decode the words and can orally explain what the reading was about but cannot write an explanation.	Can read aloud or silently and can write a brief sentence that shows some understanding of what was read.	Can read aloud or silently and can write two or more sentences that show some understanding of what was read.	Can read aloud or silently and can write a detailed explanation that shows a good understanding of what was read.

Date _____

Test score _____   Checklist Indicator(s) _____

Observation(s)

Performance Assessment
Below Expectation..Exceeds Expectations

Unable to decode the words. Cannot explain what the reading was about in any written form.	Can decode the words and can orally explain what the reading was about but cannot write an explanation.	Can read aloud or silently and can write a brief sentence that shows some understanding of what was read.	Can read aloud or silently and can write two or more sentences that show some understanding of what was read.	Can read aloud or silently and can write a detailed explanation that shows a good understanding of what was read.

Date _____

Test score _____   Checklist Indicator(s) _____

Observation(s)

Performance Assessment
Below Expectation..Exceeds Expectations

Unable to decode the words. Cannot explain what the reading was about in any written form.	Can decode the words and can orally explain what the reading was about but cannot write an explanation.	Can read aloud or silently and can write a brief sentence that shows some understanding of what was read.	Can read aloud or silently and can write two or more sentences that show some understanding of what was read.	Can read aloud or silently and can write a detailed explanation that shows a good understanding of what was read.

Summarize the Student's Response to Reading & Writing Interventions

Decision:

☐ Continue these interventions as needed and appropriate

☐ Modify the intervention:

☐ Select / implement a new intervention

☐ Move to the next tier (Tier _____)

☐ Refer for other special services:

Coil RTI Progress Monitoring Form™
Math Problem Solving

Student's Name _____

Targeted Skill, Knowledge, or Behavior
- **Correctly solves math word problems**

Pre-assessment: *(Record all that apply)*

Date(s) of Pre-assessment _____

Test score(s) _____   Checklist Indicator(s) _____

Observation(s) _____

Performance Assessment

Below Expectation...Exceeds Expectations

Uses completely incorrect procedures. Does not attempt a solution.	Uses inappropriate procedures, but does attempt a solution. Solution is incorrect.	Uses some correct procedures but solution is incomplete or partially incorrect. Steps are missing.	Uses correct procedures and has a correct solution.	Identifies all important elements of the problem. Uses correct procedures and creatively shows more than one way to solve the problem.

Strategy or Intervention: *(Describe or list below)*

Formative Assessments *(Monitoring the Student's Response to Math Problem Solving Interventions)*

Date _____

Test score _____   Checklist Indicator(s) _____

Observation(s)

Performance Assessment
Below Expectation...Exceeds Expectations

Uses completely incorrect procedures. Does not attempt a solution.	Uses inappropriate procedures, but does attempt a solution. Solution is incorrect.	Uses some correct procedures but solution is incomplete or partially incorrect. Steps are missing.	Uses correct procedures and has a correct solution.	Identifies all important elements of the problem. Uses correct procedures and creatively shows more than one way to solve the problem.

Date _____

Test score _____   Checklist Indicator(s) _____

Observation(s)

Performance Assessment
Below Expectation...Exceeds Expectations

Uses completely incorrect procedures. Does not attempt a solution.	Uses inappropriate procedures, but does attempt a solution. Solution is incorrect.	Uses some correct procedures but solution is incomplete or partially incorrect. Steps are missing.	Uses correct procedures and has a correct solution.	Identifies all important elements of the problem. Uses correct procedures and creatively shows more than one way to solve the problem.

Date _____

Test score _____   Checklist Indicator(s) _____

Observation(s)

Performance Assessment
Below Expectation...Exceeds Expectations

Uses completely incorrect procedures. Does not attempt a solution.	Uses inappropriate procedures, but does attempt a solution. Solution is incorrect.	Uses some correct procedures but solution is incomplete or partially incorrect. Steps are missing.	Uses correct procedures and has a correct solution.	Identifies all important elements of the problem. Uses correct procedures and creatively shows more than one way to solve the problem.

Summarize the Student's Response to Math Problem Solving Interventions

Decision:

☐ Continue these interventions as needed and appropriate

☐ Modify the intervention:
     ○

☐ Select / implement a new intervention

☐ Move to the next tier (Tier _____)

☐ Refer for other special services:

Coil RTI Progress Monitoring Form™
Phonemic Awareness

Student's Name _____

Targeted Skill, Knowledge, or Behavior
- **Awareness of sounds and syllables in a word**
- **Ability to distinguish the number of words in a sentence**

Pre-assessment: *(Record all that apply)*

Date(s) of Pre-assessment _____

Test score(s) _____   Checklist Indicator(s) _____

Observation(s)

Performance Assessment

Below Expectation...Exceeds Expectations

Unable to identify beginning, middle or ending sounds in a word.	Can name single vowel and consonant sounds in three-letter words.	Can name beginning, middle and ending sounds in four-letter words.	Can name sounds in words with a diagraph (2 consonants = 1 sound) or a blend (2 consonants = 2 sounds).	Can distinguish five or more sounds in a word, the number of syllables in a word, and the number of words in a sentence.

Strategies or Interventions *(Describe or list below)*

Formative Assessments *(Monitoring the Student's Response to Phonemic Awareness Interventions)*

Date _____

Test score _____   Checklist Indicator(s) _____

Observation(s)

Performance Assessment

Below Expectation...Exceeds Expectations

Unable to identify beginning, middle or ending sounds in a word.	Can name single vowel and consonant sounds in three-letter words.	Can name beginning, middle and ending sounds in four-letter words.	Can name sounds in words with a diagraph (2 consonants = 1 sound) or a blend (2 consonants = 2 sounds).	Can distinguish five or more sounds in a word, the number of syllables in a word, and the number of words in a sentence.

Date _____

Test score _____   Checklist Indicator(s) _____

Observation(s)

Performance Assessment

Below Expectation...Exceeds Expectations

Unable to identify beginning, middle or ending sounds in a word.	Can name single vowel and consonant sounds in three-letter words.	Can name beginning, middle and ending sounds in four-letter words.	Can name sounds in words with a diagraph (2 consonants = 1 sound) or a blend (2 consonants = 2 sounds).	Can distinguish five or more sounds in a word, the number of syllables in a word, and the number of words in a sentence.

Date _____

Test score _____   Checklist Indicator(s) _____

Observation(s)

Performance Assessment

Below Expectation...Exceeds Expectations

Unable to identify beginning, middle or ending sounds in a word.	Can name single vowel and consonant sounds in three-letter words.	Can name beginning, middle and ending sounds in four-letter words.	Can name sounds in words with a diagraph (2 consonants = 1 sound) or a blend (2 consonants = 2 sounds).	Can distinguish five or more sounds in a word, the number of syllables in a word, and the number of words in a sentence.

Summarize the Student's Response to Phonemic Awareness Interventions

Decision:

☐ Continue the interventions as needed and appropriate

☐ Modify the intervention:

☐ Select / implement a new intervention

☐ Move to the next tier (Tier _____)

☐ Refer for other special services:

Coil RTI Progress Monitoring Form™
Self-Esteem/Self-Confidence

Student's Name _____

Targeted Skill, Knowledge, or Behavior
- **Improve self-concept, self discipline and self-control**

Pre-assessment: *(Record all that apply)*

Date(s) of Pre-assessment _____

Test score(s) _____ Checklist Indicator(s) _____

Observation(s)

Performance Assessment

Below Expectation…………………………………………………………………………………Exceeds Expectations

Student has no confidence in himself and can see no areas of strength in either academic or personal situations.	Student sees he has one or two areas of strength and works only on those.	Student recognizes areas of weakness and sometimes uses strategies to help overcome them.	Student sometimes accomplishes tasks that require using both areas of strength and areas of weakness.	Student has confidence in himself, recognizes strengths and weaknesses, and works on turning weaknesses into strengths.

Strategies or Interventions: *(Describe or list below)*

Formative Assessments *(Monitoring the Student's Response to Self-Esteem/Self-Confidence)*

Date _____

Test score _____ Checklist Indicator(s) _____

Observation(s)

Performance Assessment

Below Expectation...Exceeds Expectations

Student has no confidence in himself and can see no areas of strength in either academic or personal situations.	Student sees he has one or two areas of strength and works only on those.	Student recognizes areas of weakness and sometimes uses strategies to help overcome them.	Student sometimes accomplishes tasks that require using both areas of strength and areas of weakness.	Student has confidence in himself, recognizes strengths and weaknesses, and works on turning weaknesses into strengths.

Date _____

Test score _____ Checklist Indicator(s) _____

Observation(s)

Performance Assessment

Below Expectation...Exceeds Expectations

Student has no confidence in himself and can see no areas of strength in either academic or personal situations.	Student sees he has one or two areas of strength and works only on those.	Student recognizes areas of weakness and sometimes uses strategies to help overcome them.	Student sometimes accomplishes tasks that require using both areas of strength and areas of weakness.	Student has confidence in himself, recognizes strengths and weaknesses, and works on turning weaknesses into strengths.

Date _____

Test score _____ Checklist Indicator(s) _____

Observation(s)

Performance Assessment

Below Expectation...Exceeds Expectations

Student has no confidence in himself and can see no areas of strength in either academic or personal situations.	Student sees he has one or two areas of strength and works only on those.	Student recognizes areas of weakness and sometimes uses strategies to help overcome them.	Student sometimes accomplishes tasks that require using both areas of strength and areas of weakness.	Student has confidence in himself, recognizes strengths and weaknesses, and works on turning weaknesses into strengths.

Summarize the Student's Response to Self-Esteem/Self-Confidence Interventions

Decision:

☐ Continue these interventions as needed and appropriate

☐ Modify the intervention:

☐ Select / implement a new intervention

☐ Move to the next tier (Tier _____)

☐ Refer for other special services:

Coil RTI Progress Monitoring Form™
Spelling & Vocabulary Patterns

Student's Name _____

Targeted Skill, Knowledge, or Behavior
- **Correctly spelling words that follow the same spelling pattern**
- **Building an understanding of the meanings of words**

Pre-assessment: *(Record all that apply)*

Date(s) of Pre-assessment _____

Test score(s) _____   Checklist Indicator(s) _____

Observation(s)

Performance Assessment

Below Expectation ....Exceeds Expectations

Does not understand that spelling patterns and word meanings have logical relationships.	Understands that words that have similar sounds often have similar spelling patterns.	Can correctly spell one-syllable words with the same spelling pattern.	Can correctly spell words of more than one syllable with the same spelling pattern.	Understands that words of more than one syllable that have the same spelling pattern may have similar meanings.

Strategies or Interventions *(Describe or list below)*

Formative Assessments *(Monitoring the Student's Response to Spelling/Vocabulary Patterns)*

Date _____

Test score _____   Checklist Indicator(s) _____

Observation(s)

Performance Assessment

Below Expectation..Exceeds Expectations

Does not understand that spelling patterns and word meanings have logical relationships.	Understands that words that have similar sounds often have similar spelling patterns.	Can correctly spell one-syllable words with the same spelling pattern.	Can correctly spell words of more than one syllable with the same spelling pattern.	Understands that words of more than one syllable that have the same spelling pattern may have similar meanings.

Date _____

Test score _____   Checklist Indicator(s) _____

Observation(s)

Performance Assessment

Below Expectation..Exceeds Expectations

Does not understand that spelling patterns and word meanings have logical relationships.	Understands that words that have similar sounds often have similar spelling patterns.	Can correctly spell one-syllable words with the same spelling pattern.	Can correctly spell words of more than one syllable with the same spelling pattern.	Understands that words of more than one syllable that have the same spelling pattern may have similar meanings.

Date _____

Test score _____   Checklist Indicator(s) _____

Observation(s)

Performance Assessment

Below Expectation..Exceeds Expectations

Does not understand that spelling patterns and word meanings have logical relationships.	Understands that words that have similar sounds often have similar spelling patterns.	Can correctly spell one-syllable words with the same spelling pattern.	Can correctly spell words of more than one syllable with the same spelling pattern.	Understands that words of more than one syllable that have the same spelling pattern may have similar meanings.

Summarize the Student's Response to Spelling & Vocabulary Patterns Interventions

Decision:

☐ Continue the interventions as needed and appropriate

☐ Modify the intervention:

☐ Select / implement a new intervention

☐ Move to the next tier (Tier _____)

☐ Refer for other special services:

Coil RTI Progress Monitoring Form™
Test-Taking Skills: Following Directions

Student's Name _____

Targeted Skill, Knowledge, or Behavior
- **Ability to follow written and oral directions when taking a test**
- **Ability to listen to oral directions and read written directions**

Pre-assessment: *(Record all that apply)*

Date(s) of Pre-assessment _____

Test score(s) _____   Checklist Indicator(s) _____

Observation(s) _____

Performance Assessment
(Below Expectation)   The more techniques circled in boxes 2-5 below, the more this skill is mastered.

Box # 1	Box # 2	Box # 3	Box # 4	Box # 5
Demonstrates no ability to listen to oral directions or read and understand written directions for the test.	Knows how to listen carefully to the details given in oral directions before and during the test.	Knows how to listen for key words in oral directions and read key words in written directions.	Pays attention to and reads sample items.	Understands what the directions say about how to mark test answers.

Strategies or Interventions *(Describe or list below)*

Intervention or Strategy   **Person Responsible**   **Timeline**

Formative Assessments *(Monitoring the Student's Response to Following Directions Interventions)*

Date _____

Test score _____   Checklist Indicator(s) _____

Observation(s)

Performance Assessment
[Below Expectation]   The more techniques circled in boxes 2-5 below, the more this skill is mastered.

Box # 1	Box # 2	Box # 3	Box # 4	Box # 5
Demonstrates no ability to listen to oral directions or read and understand written directions for the test.	Knows how to listen carefully to the details given in oral directions before and during the test.	Knows how to listen for key words in oral directions and read key words in written directions.	Pays attention to and reads sample items.	Understands what the directions say about how to mark test answers.

Date _____

Test score _____   Checklist Indicator(s) _____

Observation(s)

Performance Assessment
[Below Expectation]   The more techniques circled in boxes 2-5 below, the more this skill is mastered.

Box # 1	Box # 2	Box # 3	Box # 4	Box # 5
Demonstrates no ability to listen to oral directions or read and understand written directions for the test.	Knows how to listen carefully to the details given in oral directions before and during the test.	Knows how to listen for key words in oral directions and read key words in written directions.	Pays attention to and reads sample items.	Understands what the directions say about how to mark test answers.

Date _____

Test score _____   Checklist Indicator(s) _____

Observation(s)

Performance Assessment
[Below Expectation]   The more techniques circled in boxes 2-5 below, the more this skill is mastered.

Box # 1	Box # 2	Box # 3	Box # 4	Box # 5
Demonstrates no ability to listen to oral directions or read and understand written directions for the test.	Knows how to listen carefully to the details given in oral directions before and during the test.	Knows how to listen for key words in oral directions and read key words in written directions.	Pays attention to and reads sample items.	Understands what the directions say about how to mark test answers.

Summarize the Student's Response to Following Directions Intervention(s)

Decision:

☐ Continue the interventions as needed and appropriate

☐ Modify the intervention:

☐ Select / implement a new intervention

☐ Move to the next tier (Tier _____)

☐ Refer for other special services:

Coil RTI Progress Monitoring Form™
Test-Taking Skills: Multiple Choice Questions

Student's Name _____

Targeted Skill, Knowledge, or Behavior
- **Ability to understand and answer multiple choice questions**
- **Knowledge of techniques for answering multiple choice questions**

Pre-assessment: *(Record all that apply)*

Date(s) of Pre-assessment _____

Test score(s) _____   Checklist Indicator(s) _____

Observation(s)

Performance Assessment
(Below Expectation) The more techniques circled in boxes 2-5 below, the more this skill is mastered.

Box # 1	Box # 2	Box # 3	Box # 4	Box # 5
Does not understand how multiple choice questions work and has no system for answering them.	Understands the importance of reading all the choices before answering the question.	Understands the need to eliminate answers that are obviously wrong.	Understands how to eliminate answers that are only partially correct.	Looks for key phrases such as "all of the above," "all of these except," "none of the above."

Strategies or Interventions *(Describe or list below)*

Intervention or Strategy   **Person Responsible**   **Timeline**

Formative Assessments *(Monitoring the Student's Response to Answering Multiple Choice Questions Interventions)*

Date _____

Test score _____   Checklist Indicator(s) _____

Observation(s)

Performance Assessment
[Below Expectation]   The more techniques circled in boxes 2-5 below, the more this skill is mastered.

Box # 1	Box # 2	Box # 3	Box # 4	Box # 5
Does not understand how multiple choice questions work and has no system for answering them.	Understands the importance of reading all the choices before answering the question.	Understands the need to eliminate answers that are obviously wrong.	Understands how to eliminate answers that are only partially correct.	Looks for key phrases such as "all of the above," "all of these except," "none of the above."

Date _____

Test score _____   Checklist Indicator(s) _____

Observation(s)

Performance Assessment
[Below Expectation]   The more techniques circled in boxes 2-5 below, the more this skill is mastered.

Box # 1	Box # 2	Box # 3	Box # 4	Box # 5
Does not understand how multiple choice questions work and has no system for answering them.	Understands the importance of reading all the choices before answering the question.	Understands the need to eliminate answers that are obviously wrong.	Understands how to eliminate answers that are only partially correct.	Looks for key phrases such as "all of the above," "all of these except," "none of the above."

Date _____

Test score _____   Checklist Indicator(s) _____

Observation(s)

Performance Assessment
[Below Expectation]   The more techniques circled in boxes 2-5 below, the more this skill is mastered.

Box # 1	Box # 2	Box # 3	Box # 4	Box # 5
Does not understand how multiple choice questions work and has no system for answering them.	Understands the importance of reading all the choices before answering the question.	Understands the need to eliminate answers that are obviously wrong.	Understands how to eliminate answers that are only partially correct.	Looks for key phrases such as "all of the above," "all of these except," "none of the above."

**Summarize the Student's Response to Answering Multiple Choice Questions
Intervention(s)**

Decision:

☐ Continue the interventions as needed and appropriate

☐ Modify the intervention:

☐ Select / implement a new intervention

☐ Move to the next tier (Tier _____)

☐ Refer for other special services:

Coil RTI Progress Monitoring Form™
Test-Taking Skills: Reading the Questions

Student's Name _____

Targeted Skill, Knowledge, or Behavior
- **Ability to read test questions accurately**
- **Ability to understand what the test questions are asking**

Pre-assessment: *(Record all that apply)*

Date(s) of Pre-assessment _____

Test score(s) _____   Checklist Indicator(s) _____

Observation(s)

Performance Assessment

(Below Expectation) The more techniques circled in boxes 2-5 below, the more this skill is mastered.

Box # 1	Box # 2	Box # 3	Box # 4	Box # 5
Demonstrates no ability to read test questions accurately or interpret what the questions are asking.	Can read the questions to find key words or familiar words.	Is able to put test questions in his/her own words.	Understands not to read things that aren't there into the questions.	Uses general knowledge about the topic to better understand the test questions.

Strategies or Interventions *(Describe or list below)*

Intervention or Strategy   **Person Responsible**   **Timeline**

Formative Assessments *(Monitoring the Student's Response to Reading the Questions Interventions)*

Date _____

Test score _____   Checklist Indicator(s) _____

Observation(s)

Performance Assessment
[Below Expectation]   The more techniques circled in boxes 2-5 below, the more this skill is mastered.

Box # 1	Box # 2	Box # 3	Box # 4	Box # 5
Demonstrates no ability to read test questions accurately or interpret what the questions are asking.	Can read the questions to find key words or familiar words.	Is able to put test questions in his/her own words.	Understands not to read things that aren't there into the questions.	Uses general knowledge about the topic to better understand the test questions.

Date _____

Test score _____   Checklist Indicator(s) _____

Observation(s)

Performance Assessment
[Below Expectation]   The more techniques circled in boxes 2-5 below, the more this skill is mastered.

Box # 1	Box # 2	Box # 3	Box # 4	Box # 5
Demonstrates no ability to read test questions accurately or interpret what the questions are asking.	Can read the questions to find key words or familiar words.	Is able to put test questions in his/her own words.	Understands not to read things that aren't there into the questions.	Uses general knowledge about the topic to better understand the test questions.

Date _____

Test score _____   Checklist Indicator(s) _____

Observation(s)

Performance Assessment
[Below Expectation]   The more techniques circled in boxes 2-5 below, the more this skill is mastered.

Box # 1	Box # 2	Box # 3	Box # 4	Box # 5
Demonstrates no ability to read test questions accurately or interpret what the questions are asking.	Can read the questions to find key words or familiar words.	Is able to put test questions in his/her own words.	Understands not to read things that aren't there into the questions.	Uses general knowledge about the topic to better understand the test questions.

Summarize the Student's Response to Reading the Questions Intervention(s)

Decision:

☐ Continue the interventions as needed and appropriate

☐ Modify the intervention:

☐ Select / implement a new intervention

☐ Move to the next tier (Tier _____)

☐ Refer for other special services:

Coil RTI Progress Monitoring Form™
Test-Taking Skills: Time Management Techniques

Student's Name _____

Targeted Skill, Knowledge, or Behavior
- **Ability to use time wisely when taking a test**
- **Ability to pace oneself appropriately when taking a test**

Pre-assessment: *(Record all that apply)*

Date(s) of Pre-assessment _____

Test score(s) _____   Checklist Indicator(s) _____

Observation(s)

Performance Assessment
(Below Expectation) The more techniques circled in boxes 2-5 below, the more this skill is mastered.

Box # 1	Box # 2	Box # 3	Box # 4	Box # 5
Demonstrates no ability to use time wisely during a test and cannot pace himself to get finished in time.	Looks over entire test first to judge approximately how much time each item should take.	Does not spend too much time on any one test item but also does not rush through the test.	Keeps track of time as he/she is taking the test.	Unless there is a penalty for doing this, the student guesses at answers he doesn't know and writes them just before the test time is up.

Strategies or Interventions *(Describe or list below)*

Intervention or Strategy   **Person Responsible**   **Timeline**

Formative Assessments *(Monitoring the Student's Response to Test-taking Time Management Interventions)*

Date _____

Test score _____   Checklist Indicator(s) _____

Observation(s)

Performance Assessment

[Below Expectation]   The more techniques circled in boxes 2-5 below, the more this skill is mastered.

Box # 1	Box # 2	Box # 3	Box # 4	Box # 5
Demonstrates no ability to use time wisely during a test and cannot pace himself to get finished in time.	Looks over entire test first to judge approximately how much time each item should take.	Does not spend too much time on any one test item but also does not rush through the test.	Keeps track of time as he/she is taking the test.	Unless there is a penalty for doing this, the student guesses at answers he doesn't know and writes them just before the test time is up.

Date _____

Test score _____   Checklist Indicator(s) _____

Observation(s)

Performance Assessment

[Below Expectation]   The more techniques circled in boxes 2-5 below, the more this skill is mastered.

Box # 1	Box # 2	Box # 3	Box # 4	Box # 5
Demonstrates no ability to use time wisely during a test and cannot pace himself to get finished in time.	Looks over entire test first to judge approximately how much time each item should take.	Does not spend too much time on any one test item but also does not rush through the test.	Keeps track of time as he/she is taking the test.	Unless there is a penalty for doing this, the student guesses at answers he doesn't know and writes them just before the test time is up.

Date _____

Test score _____   Checklist Indicator(s) _____

Observation(s)

Performance Assessment

[Below Expectation]   The more techniques circled in boxes 2-5 below, the more this skill is mastered.

Box # 1	Box # 2	Box # 3	Box # 4	Box # 5
Demonstrates no ability to use time wisely during a test and cannot pace himself to get finished in time.	Looks over entire test first to judge approximately how much time each item should take.	Does not spend too much time on any one test item but also does not rush through the test.	Keeps track of time as he/she is taking the test.	Unless there is a penalty for doing this, the student guesses at answers he doesn't know and writes them just before the test time is up.

Summarize the Student's Response to
Test-taking Time Management Techniques Intervention(s)

Decision:

☐ Continue the interventions as needed and appropriate

☐ Modify the intervention:

☐ Select / implement a new intervention

☐ Move to the next tier (Tier _____)

☐ Refer for other special services:

Introduction to Ready-to-Use Checklists, Forms, and Assessments

Throughout this book you have seen a variety of checklists, forms, and assessments that have been used with students. This section of the book contains these forms to use with your students.

All are reproducible and can be printed directly from the CD. Some of the forms are also appropriate for you to write on or complete with your own lessons or information. The following forms can be found in this section of the book:

- ☐ Curriculum Compactor
- ☐ Goal Setting: Where Do You Want To Go – How Do You Plan To Get There?
- ☐ Mindmap – Goal Setting, Problem Solving and Decision Making
- ☐ Concept Map
- ☐ Storyboard Visual Organizer
- ☐ Compare/Contrast - Venn diagram
- ☐ Learning Preferences Checklist
- ☐ Learning Styles Checklist
- ☐ Learning Modalities Checklist
- ☐ Listening Skills Checklist
- ☐ RTI Achievement Characteristics Checklist
- ☐ RTI Behavioral Characteristics Checklist
- ☐ RTI Organization Checklist
- ☐ Tiered Lesson Planning forms and instructions for writing your own
- ☐ Individual Lesson Plan™ forms and instructions for writing your own
- ☐ Product Criteria Cards

CURRICULUM COMPACTOR FORM

Student's Name _____

Skill, Knowledge, Benchmark or Standard	Documentation of Mastery	Student Choice Alternate Activities

from Successful Teaching in the Differentiated Classroom. Carolyn Coil.
Pieces of Learning. www.piecesoflearning.com

GOAL SETTING

WHERE DO YOU WANT TO GO – HOW DO YOU PLAN TO GET THERE?

1. What school-related goals will you work toward during the next grading period?

How will you achieve these goals?

a. _____   _____

b. _____   _____

c. _____   _____

During this school year?

a. _____   _____

b. _____   _____

After high school?

a. _____   _____

b. _____   _____

2. What personal goals would you like to achieve in the next 6 months?

How will you achieve these goals?

a. _____   _____

b. _____   _____

c. _____   _____

Within the next year or two?

a. _____   _____

b. _____   _____

from Becoming an Achiever. Carolyn Coil. Pieces of Learning. www.piecesoflearning.com

MINDMAP - PROBLEM SOLVING, GOAL SETTING
& DECISION MAKING

Complete the circles with your goal and steps to achieve it. Then number the circles in the order you need to attack your goal.

from Becoming an Achiever. Carolyn Coil. Pieces of Learning. www.piecesoflearning.com

CONCEPT MAP

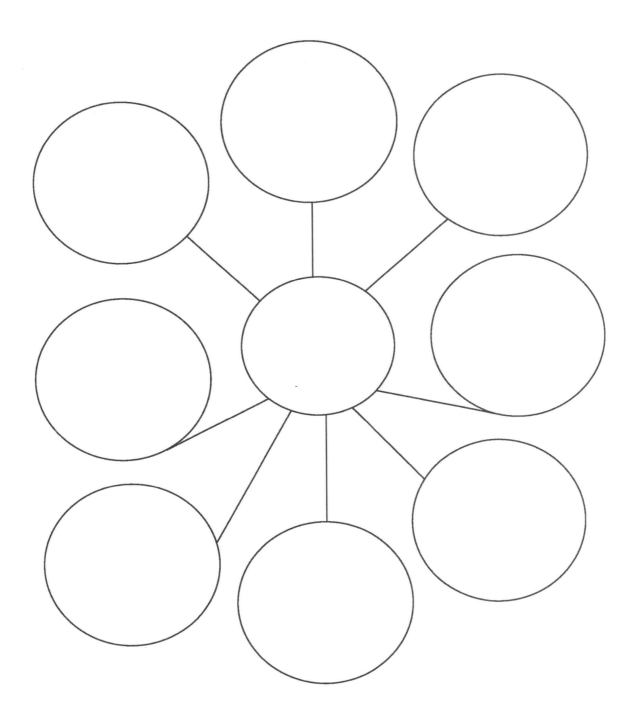

Story Board Visual Organizer

Put events in the right order.

Title of Story

1st	2nd	3rd

4th	5th	6th

Compare and Contrast
VENN DIAGRAM

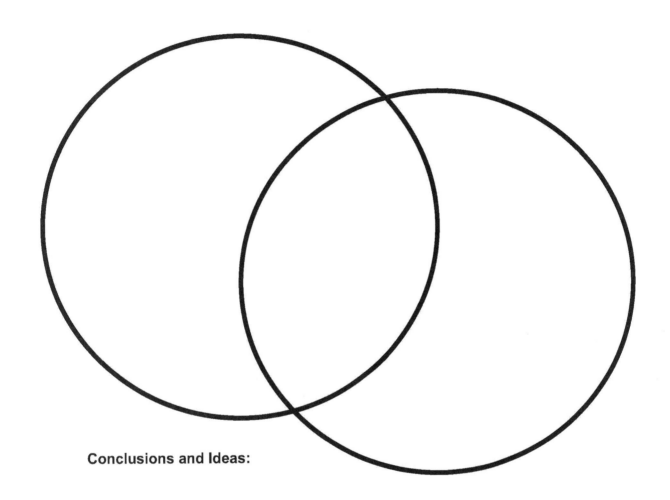

Conclusions and Ideas:

from Teaching Tools for the 21st Century. Carolyn Coil.
Pieces of Learning. www.piecesoflearning.com

Learning Profiles and Preferences Checklist

Write the names of students that come to mind for each of the learning preferences below.

Visual learners: _____
- o Learn by seeing, watching demonstrations
- o Enjoy and learn from visual displays and colors
- o Like pictures, graphic organizers, maps, storyboards

Verbal learners: _____
- o Enjoy listening and are always ready to talk
- o Like music, poetry, dialogues, skits, and debates
- o Learn through verbal instructions

Kinesthetic learners: _____
- o Learn by hands-on experiences
- o Like working with materials, manipulatives, and tools
- o Remember what they have done more than what they have seen or heard

Technological learners: _____
- o Know how to use technological tools without formal instruction
- o Expertise in using digital cameras, video production tools, smart boards, computer technologies
- o Understand how to integrate various technologies

Musical/Rhythmic learners: _____
- o Have the ability to communicate through music and poetry
- o Can compose and / or perform musically
- o Have a natural rhythm, beat, and harmony

Logical/Mathematical learners: _____
- o Think in a logical, ordered, sequential way
- o Use reasoning and logic to solve problems
- o Use numbers effectively
- o See logical patterns, statements, and relationships

Naturalist learners: _____
- o Can create categories and sort / index items accordingly
- o Are able to recognize and make distinctions between things in nature
- o Observe things in nature others would miss

Intrapersonal/Reflective learners: _____
- o Recognize their own strengths and weaknesses
- o Learn from successes and failures
- o Plan for and uses suitable organization and study skills
- o Understand their own hopes, dreams, aspirations, and emotions

Interpersonal / Group Oriented learners: _____
- o Work well as a member of groups
- o Are able to lead and persuade others
- o Respond appropriately to both verbal and non-verbal cues from others
- o Consider advice and opinions of others when making a decision

LEARNING STYLES CHECKLIST

Concrete sequential students like to:

_____ Read or listen to, and then follow directions.

_____ Take notes, look at charts or diagrams, and do outlines.

_____ Participate in structured learning, including pencil and paper exercises.

_____ Have an organized teacher.

_____ Know what the marking system is and what the teacher's specific expectations.

Abstract sequential students like to:

_____ Read different kinds of books, usually from beginning to end sequentially.

_____ Listen to audio tapes, compact disks and lectures, see videos, films and slides, and work on the computer and other electronic learning tools.

_____ Help other students understand the subject matter or what they've read.

_____ Find THE answer to a problem, but are uncomfortable with multiple answers and possibilities.

_____ Look at things logically, even situations where a logical solution is not necessarily the best one or does not solve the problem.

Concrete random students like to:

_____ Complete a product or project for a classroom assignment.

_____ Brainstorm creative ideas.

_____ Take risks. Concrete random students will volunteer for anything!

_____ Do things by trial and error.

_____ Solve problems alone.

_____ Avoid IQ and achievement tests.

Abstract random students like to:

_____ Listen to, learn from, and respond to their classmates.

_____ Work in groups and will become the natural leaders in small groups.

_____ Do short reading assignments and often do not read books sequentially.

_____ Use emotions and intuition.

_____ Have lots of things going on at once.

from Motivating Underachievers. Carolyn Coil. Pieces of Learning. www.piecesoflearning.com

LEARNING MODALITIES CHECKLIST

Check items in each category that describe an individual student. The strongest learning modality or modalities will be those with the most items checked.

Student Name _____

Visual learners

❑ Are good with detail

❑ Learn by seeing, watching demonstrations

❑ Often remember whatever they have written down

❑ Can recall the placement of words and pictures on a page

❑ Like descriptive reading

❑ Enjoy and learn from visual displays and colors

❑ Recognize words by sight and people by face rather than name

❑ Have a vivid imagination and think in pictures

❑ Are deliberate problem solvers and plan solutions in advance

❑ Facial expressions are a good indication of their emotions

Auditory/Verbal learners

❑ Enjoy listening but are always ready to talk

❑ Like music, rap, poetry, rhyming words

❑ Enjoy dialogues, skits and debates

❑ Have auditory word attack skills and learn words phonetically

❑ Talk to themselves, repeating information aloud

❑ Are distracted by sounds

❑ Talk out problems and the pros and cons of a situation

❑ Express emotion through changes in pitch, tone and volume of voice

❑ Are not detail persons; tend to be global thinkers

❑ Learn through verbal instructions from others or themselves

from Motivating Underachievers. Carolyn Coil. Pieces of Learning. www.piecesoflearning.com

Kinesthetic/Tactile learners

❑ Learn by hands-on experiences

❑ Prefer direct involvement rather than being a spectator

❑ Enjoy the performing arts and/or athletics

❑ Like working with materials, machinery and tools

❑ Prefer action/adventure stories and videos

❑ Communicate feelings through body language

❑ Experiment with ideas to see how they will work in the real world

❑ Touch, feel, manipulate, and play with objects

❑ Show emotions physically by jumping, hugging, applauding, etc.

❑ Remember what they have done rather than what they have seen or read

Technological learners

❑ Are mechanically oriented

❑ Know how to use technological tools without formal instruction

❑ Enjoy using a video camera

❑ Obtain much of their information electronically

❑ Like integrated learning activities

❑ Would like to learn everything via the computer

❑ Spend much of their spare time on the computer or playing video games

❑ Know how to work with and use new software and hardware

❑ Interact and communicate with others via the Internet

❑ Understand how to integrate various technologies

from Motivating Underachievers. Carolyn Coil. Pieces of Learning. www.piecesoflearning.com

Listening Skills for Group Work Checklist

Student's Name _____

Directions:

*Mark **YES** or **NO** for each item. Items marked **NO** are those the student needs to work on.*

— 1.   Student listens quietly while other group members are talking.

— 2.   Student avoids carrying on side conversations while the group is meeting.

— 3.   Student monitors the noise level of his/her group and the class as a whole and tells the teacher if the noise gets too loud.

— 4.   Student adds his/her own ideas to what others have said.

— 5.   Student asks for clarification when he/she doesn't understand another person's ideas.

— 6.   Student accepts the ideas of others even when he disagrees.

— 7.   Student concentrates on what other people in the group are saying.

— 8.   Student does not interrupt while someone else is talking.

— 9.   Student can summarize the main points of content and knowledge in a group discussion and asks if this is correct.

— 10. Student can summarize what the group has done and said at the end of the group session.

RTI Achievement Characteristics Checklist

Directions: *Rate the targeted student using the following indicators.*
You may leave some items blank.

W =	Weak in this area
I =	Improving in this area
S =	Strong in this area

Name of student: _____

— 1.   Exhibits good organizational and time management skills.

— 2.   Turns assignments in on time.

— 3.   Is punctual and has good attendance.

— 4.   Is persistent when working on tasks that don't come easily.

— 5.   Is willing to redo work when it is not correct the first time.

— 6.   Shows pride in the quality of his/her schoolwork.

— 7.   Is willing to obtain help in remediation of an academic weakness.

— 8.   Works to improve when grades or test scores are low.

— 9.   Finds at least one topic/subject at school that he/she feels is interesting and worthwhile.

— 10.   Knows strategies for memorizing unfamiliar information.

— 11. Has a good attention span and can concentrate on learning.

— 12. Shows creativity at home or at school.

— 13. Can think logically to solve academic problems.

— 14. Sets short- and long-term goals.

— 15. Sees the relationship between achievement in school and future success.

Specific behaviors can be identified and targeted by using this checklist. You can also identify patterns of positive or negative behaviors.

RTI Behavioral Characteristics Checklist

Directions: *Rate the targeted student using the following indicators. You may leave some items blank.*

W =	Weak in this area
I =	Improving in this area
S =	Strong in this area

Name of student: _____

— 1. Has a high, yet realistic self-concept.

— 2. Practices self-discipline and self control.

— 3. Has a positive attitude about school.

— 4.   Attempts to display appropriate behavior in school.

— 5. Listens to those in authority over him/her.

— 6. Communicates problems and concerns to teachers and others in authority

— 7. Works to turn failures into successes.

— 8. Can see that failures are opportunities for learning.

— 9. Exhibits flexible thinking about his/her behavior and problems.

— 10. Takes responsibility for problems and does not put all the blame on others.

— 11. Recognizes his/her contribution to negative situations.

— 12. Functions well in a group working on a constructive project.

— 13. Has a close friend(s) with whom he/she shares similar (socially acceptable)

        interests.

— 14. Has friends who are achievers and have positive attitudes about school.

— 15. Uses influence over others in a positive way.

Specific behaviors can be identified and targeted by using this checklist. You can also identify patterns of positive or negative behaviors.

RTI Organization Checklist

Directions: *Mark a check under* **Yes** *or* **No** *to indicate how organized this student is.*

Name of student: _____

No	**Yes**	
___	___	1. There are things in his/her locker, backpack, desk, or cubby that haven't been looked at in a month or more.
___	___	2. At home, she/he has a pile of books, comic books, magazines, or videos that have been recorded that she/he hasn't read or seen yet but is going to do some day.
___	___	3. This student never writes down assignments because he/she thinks he/she can remember everything that is important.
___	___	4. He/she forgets about long-range assignments until it's too late to do a good job on them.
___	___	5. This student's parents keep track of his/her schedule of after-school activities, and the student just does whatever they tell him/her to do.
___	___	6. Once a week or more, this student leaves at home at least one of the following: materials needed for class, homework, notes that should be signed, agenda books, etc.
___	___	7. This student has a hard time keeping track of his/her keys, glasses, purse, wallet, jacket, shoes, hat, or other things he/she can't leave home or school without.
___	___	8. This student has trouble remembering important dates like anniversaries, birthdays, class field trips, test dates, etc.
___	___	9. When this student starts on an assignment or project, he/she has a hard time completing it because of getting distracted easily.
___	___	10. This student is very disorganized but is motivated to learn organizational skills.
___	___	Totals

SCORING

10, 9 or 8	Yes – This student has major problems with organization!
7 or 6	Yes – This student needs to develop additional organizational skills.
5, 4 or 3	Yes – This student has good organizational skills but can still improve.
2, 1 or 0	Yes – This student has excellent organizational skills!

This checklist helps to pinpoint areas where students need assistance in becoming more organized. If you look at the items marked "Yes," you will see which areas are organizational problems for an individual student.

Tiered Activities

Writing Tiered Lessons or Units

Writing tiered lessons and units can be challenging. Below are some steps to guide your planning. Use the blank Tiered Lesson form on the next page to write your own Tiered Lessons or Unit.

1. Establish which standards, objectives, knowledge or skills all students need to know at the end of this lesson or unit. Use your state's standards documents to guide you.

2. Think about activities you have done with students in the past to reach these standards or objectives. Brainstorm with other teachers and use your resources to get other ideas. Use the Initial Planning Form to make a list of activities. Write each activity on the first line for each item on the form.

3. Decide which are appropriate learning activities for all students. These will become your whole class activities. Label these **WC**.

4. Some of the activities on your list will most likely be easier than others. Label the level or tier you think each activity might be. Consider your class and decide on how many levels you need to have. I usually have two or three levels.

5. Think about ways to expand or extend the easier activities so they will be challenging for higher ability students, and ways to simplify the more difficult activities so that your struggling students can do them successfully.

6. Look carefully at your list of activities. Many times you will have more activities than you could possibly do given the amount of time you have for the unit. Decide which activities are essential and which could be eliminated if necessary. You may want to save a couple of activities to use as anchoring activities with students at any level who finish their work before others.

7. Check again to make sure all activities will lead to students learning the standards and objectives.

8. Make certain that activities at all levels are engaging and interesting. Nothing discourages achievement faster than students thinking that the other group is the one with the fun, interesting or enjoyable activity while the learning activity they have been assigned is not.

9. Write your unit or lesson plan using the Tiered Lesson Plan format.

10. Check to see that the activities at one level are parallel to the ones done at another level. For example, are all students creating a visual or are all students doing research? Tiered lessons are easiest to implement when activities at all levels are similar to one another.

11. Plan daily lessons based on your tiered lesson or unit plan.

12. As you would with any lesson or unit, gather supplies and resources needed to do the activities.

from Successful Teaching in the Differentiated Classroom. Carolyn Coil.
Pieces of Learning. www.piecesoflearning.com

Tiered Activities

Initial Planning Form for a Tiered Unit

Theme or Topic:_____

Standards/Benchmarks:_____
_____
_____
_____

Possible Student Activities   **Levels of Difficulty**

1. _____   _____

   _____   _____

   _____   _____

2. _____   _____

   _____   _____

   _____   _____

3. _____   _____

   _____   _____

   _____   _____

4. _____   _____

   _____   _____

   _____   _____

5. _____   _____

   _____   _____

   _____   _____

6. _____   _____

   _____   _____

   _____   _____

from Successful Teaching in the Differentiated Classroom. Carolyn Coil.
Pieces of Learning. www.piecesoflearning.com

Tiered Lesson Plan: Unit Planning Form

_____

Objectives or Standards

1.

2.

3.

4.

Whole Class Activities

Assessment

Level 1 Activities

Assessment

from Activities & Assessments for the Differentiated Classroom. Carolyn Coil.
Pieces of Learning. www.piecesoflearning.com

Level 2 Activities

Assessment

Level 3 Activities

Assessment

Whole Class Culminating Activities

Assessment

from Activities & Assessments for the Differentiated Classroom. Carolyn Coil.
Pieces of Learning. www.piecesoflearning.com

Individual Lesson Plan

Steps to Develop an ILP™

___1. Decide on a major theme or topic for the unit.

___2. Generate a unit rationale, a broad list of essential questions, objectives, and outcomes, and the enduring understandings you hope will result from the unit.

___3. List unit objectives/outcomes and state standards for the unit.

___4. Brainstorm a list of possible unit activities. Use your textbook, supplemental resources, Internet websites, and other teachers to help generate ideas.

___5. Categorize each activity according to learning preferences/profiles (see Chapter 5), content areas or in any other category you want.

___6. Decide which will be Student Choice activities and which will be required of all students.

___7. Use the Individual Lesson Plan (ILP™) format to organize your unit activities.

___8. Include one independent activity in the activities required of all students. List this activity first in the 'Required Activities – Teacher's Choice' section of the ILP™. This will be what all students can work on while you are meeting with small groups of students and discussing their Student Choice activities.

___9. Write all Teacher Required Activities in the upper right hand quadrant of the ILP™. Include products or performances and assessment criteria for each.

___10. Write all Student Choice activities in consecutive numerical order for easy reference. This way, you can keep a record of which students have chosen which activity by recording the number of the activity on the Activity Chart.

___11. Find or develop resources and materials needed for the unit.

___12. Develop assessments to assess unit objectives, outcomes, and standards. You could develop complete rubrics, mini-rubrics, tests or quizzes, observation logs, charts, and a host of other assessment instruments.

___13. As you would with any unit, develop daily lesson plans based on your unit plan.

from Successful Teaching in the Differentiated Classroom. Carolyn Coil.
Pieces of Learning. www.piecesoflearning.com

Individual Lesson Plan

ILP™ Unit Planner

Topic or Theme_____

What do I want my students to know about this topic? What are the essential questions we want to answer? What are the Big Ideas?

- _____
- _____
- _____
- _____

What state standards are we working to meet?

- _____
- _____
- _____
- _____

Student Activities	Product/ Performance	Learning Preference/ Category
1. _____	_____	_____
2. _____	_____	_____
3. _____	_____	_____
4. _____	_____	_____
5. _____	_____	_____
6. _____	_____	_____
7. _____	_____	_____
8. _____	_____	_____
9. _____	_____	_____
10. _____	_____	_____
11._____	_____	_____

from Successful Teaching in the Differentiated Classroom. Carolyn Coil.
Pieces of Learning. www.piecesoflearning.com

Individual Lesson Plan –

Required Activities Teacher's Choice	Product/Performance Required	Assessment – Required Activities

Standards/Objectives:

Student Choices in Ways to Learn	Product/Performance Student Choice	Due Dates Student Choice Activities
Choice Category #1 _____ Choice Category #2 _____ Choice Category #3 _____ Choice Category #4 _____		

Carolyn Coil, www.carolyncoil.com

ACTIVITIES – STUDENT CHOICES

Choice Category #1	Choice Category #2
Choice Category #3	**Choice Category #4**

from <u>*Successful Teaching in the Differentiated Classroom*</u>. *Carolyn Coil.*
Pieces of Learning. www.piecesoflearning.com

194

Assessment of Student Choices _____

Unit _____

1. _____

• • • •

Possible points = ___

2. _____

• • • •

Possible points = ___

3. _____

• • • •

Possible points = ___

4. _____

• • • •

Possible points = ___

5. _____

• • • •

Possible points = ___

6. _____

• • • •

Possible points = ___

7. _____

• • • •

Possible points = ___

8. _____

• • • •

Possible points = ___

from Successful Teaching in the Differentiated Classroom. Carolyn Coil.
Pieces of Learning. www.piecesoflearning.com

Product Criteria Cards

Diorama	Poster
1. Realistic depiction of scene	1. On poster board
2. Sides have background scenery	2. Legible, neat writing
3. 3-dimensional figures/objects in foreground	3. Has visuals about topic
4. Durable construction	4. Has title and labels spelled correctly
5. Accurate	5. Neat with white space
Graph	**Song**
1. Labels/Title	1. Appropriate content
2. Accurate data plotted correctly	2. Has a rhythm
3. Ruled measurements	3. Words and music go together
4. Easy to understand	4. Can be sung; auditory appeal
5. Neatness	
Oral Presentation/Report	**Short Story**
1. Clear speaking loud enough for all to hear	1. Has a beginning, middle, and end
2. Good eye contact	2. Has at least one character
3. Uses gestures and visuals	3. Setting is appropriate for the story
4. Correct timing	4. Plot and actions are understandable
	5. Correct spelling, punctuation, and grammar

Criteria cards are wonderful assessment shortcuts. They list generic attributes of products or processes that students can use over and over again regardless of the academic content they are studying. These cards are short, easily understood lists of criteria (generally 4 or 5 items) that students can refer to each time they do the same product or process.

Using criteria cards is an excellent intervention for many students. They make the teacher's expectations clear and, when used by several teachers, provide consistency and clarity over time. This is very beneficial to many students because they don't have to wonder what each teacher means when assigning similar tasks.

In mini-rubrics, short lists of criteria such as the ones used to assess an ILP™ (form found on the previous page), and in larger complex rubrics, criteria cards help teachers concentrate on the knowledge and academic skills learned rather than the student's skill in constructing a beautiful product. Criteria cards generally count as 25% of the grade and the knowledge the student shows via the product counts for 75%. Use the form on the next page to write your own criteria cards.

Criteria Cards

Product and Process Criteria Card: Write Your Own

from Successful Teaching in the Differentiated Classroom. Carolyn Coil.
Pieces of Learning. www.piecesoflearning.com

Afterword

There are literally hundreds of research-based interventions to use with students when implementing an RTI plan. In this book I have shown you examples of students and the strategies/interventions that were tried with them. In most cases I have also included forms, checklists, lesson plans, etc. As you can see by looking at the *Coil RTI Progress Monitoring Forms*™ used with individual students, some interventions brought great progress, others worked to some degree, and still others were not effective at all.

One of the things I discovered is that the interventions tend to fall into one of two categories. Some interventions are specific strategies for differentiated instruction. Others are more general strategies to help students with motivation, behavior, and academic growth.

Over the past fifteen years, I have written a number of books that address these issues and ideas. All of my books are filled with research-based strategies and interventions that can be used with your RTI plan of action. My books, which are listed below, should be helpful to you as you seek ways to work with your students. All are published by Pieces of Learning and can be obtained by logging onto the Pieces of Learning website at www.piecesoflearning.com. Details about each are below.

- *Becoming an Achiever* – This book is a student handbook appropriate for students 4th grade and above. It covers strategies for building self-confidence, goal setting, self-motivation, time management and organization, study skills, test-taking skills, and learning to deal with the system.

- *Encouraging Achievement* – This book has over 150 strategies and interventions to help students achieve. Chapters include the role of the school, the role of the home, the role of society, stress management, teaching responsibility and persistence, independent learning, and creative lesson planning.

- *Motivating Underachievers* – This book has 220 strategies and interventions to use with your students. Each is practical and doable and has the potential to motivate your underachievers and increase achievement in your targeted RTI students. Some schools use this as their handbook of research-based ideas for RTI interventions.

- *Teaching Tools for the 21st Century* – A research-based book that considers many of the major educational theories and ideas of the past 30 years and explains how to use these theories to help students. Included are ideas and interventions about learning styles, learning modalities, Bloom's Taxonomy, multiple intelligences, gifted students, students with disabilities, cultural and linguistic diversity, dealing with conflict, using technology, and working with parents.

- **Standards-Based Activities & Assessments for the Differentiated Classroom** – This book has 49 differentiated units of work with all of the activities and all of the assessments written and ready-to-use. These units cover many content areas. Each unit is written in one of three formats: tiered lessons and units, tic-tac-toe, or the Individual Lesson Plan ™ format. Using these differentiated units is an appropriate intervention for many students.

- **Solving the Assessment Puzzle** – This book covers everything you need to know about educational assessment. Included is assessment terminology, standards, standardized testing, alternative assessments, how to write rubrics, the link between instruction and assessment, pre-assessment, formative assessment, and summative assessment. The final third of the book has 75 rubrics that are already written and ready-to-use. Using such rubrics is a good way to monitor student progress on a wide range of products and performances.

- **Successful Teaching in the Differentiated Classroom** – This user-friendly book is filled with strategies for differentiating curriculum and instruction. Nearly all of the strategies in this book are also excellent research-based interventions. Included are curriculum compacting, flexible grouping, independent study, resident experts, literature circles, learning centers, learning contracts, learning preferences, higher-level questioning, computer assisted instruction, and more.

- **Coil RTI Progress Monitoring Forms™ for Gifted Learners**
  Coil RTI Progress Monitoring Forms™ for Struggling Learners
  These two packets have hard copies and a customizable CD for all of the Progress Monitoring Forms. You can change the wording on any of the forms or print and use them as written.

I hope that this book is helpful to you as you seek new ways to help your students. Print and complete the appropriate reproducible RTI forms as you monitor the progress of any student. Share your results with other teachers, your school RTI team, the student, and/or the parents as is suitable.

Using these targeted pre-assessments and formative assessments will help students and teachers see when progress is being made and will also show when an intervention is ineffective and needs to be changed. Don't hesitate to change an intervention that is not working as you thought it would. There are many interventions, approaches, and strategies to try, so don't continue with an unsuccessful one! Find the interventions that work best for each student, and use them accordingly. In this way your students will become successful lifelong learners and productive citizens in the 21st century.